HEBREW GOSPEL

Scholars Comparing Texts,
from Folio 37v of the Darmstadt Haggadah, 15th cent. C.E.

HEBREW GOSPEL

Cracking the Code of Mark

Wolfgang Roth

WIPF & STOCK · Eugene, Oregon

Wipf and Stock Publishers
199 W 8th Ave, Suite 3
Eugene, OR 97401

Hebrew Gospel
Cracking the Code of Mark
By Roth, Wolfgang
Copyright©1988 by Roth, Wolfgang
ISBN 13: 978-1-60899-158-7
Publication date 10/22/2009
Previously published by Meyer Stone, 1988

To
Janet Pearson Roth
fellow sojourner on many paths

Contents

Preface

"There is no real analogy to his [Mark's] gospel as a literary whole." Kee's words (30) summarize the present consensus, echoing Wilder's dictum formulated some twenty years ago: The genre of the gospel "is the only wholly new genre created by the Church and the author of Mark receives the credit for it" (36).

My research into the compositional structure and narrative execution of early Jewish and Christian writings has persuaded me that there is evidence to the contrary. This study advances the thesis that Mark's work is basically, though not exclusively, patterned by a narrative of similar plot, cast, and volume present in that body of literature that is the primary matrix of early Christian reflection and writing: the Hebrew Scriptures.

Thus it is my goal to show how the appearance of Jesus, the martyr from Nazareth, was conceptualized and narrated by the second evangelist in the light of that paradigm, and to discuss the nature of the hermeneutic activity that, following scriptural codes, generated the gospel of Mark.

I am grateful to several colleagues who have discussed my approach and findings with me in the course of the journey of this study through earlier versions, especially Phyllis Bird, Robert L. Cohn, Robert Jewett, S. Dean McBride, Jr., Vernon

K. Robbins, and Lou H. Silberman. Their observations and counsels do of course not implicate them in my thesis and its argumentation.

WOLFGANG ROTH

Evanston, Illinois
November 7, 1987

Chapter 1

Introduction

1.1 Beyond Elijah's Return

"Elijah must come first...." This is the expectation that Peter, James, and John quote to Jesus as they make their way down from the Mount of Transfiguration. Their master agrees. He not only adds that the man of Tishbe, on his return to the terrestrial sphere, "restores all things," but also observes that this has already happened. With evident reference to John the Baptist's activity and martyrdom, Jesus says that "they did to him as they pleased, as it is written concerning him" (Mk 9:11–13).

The anticipation that Jesus and the three disciples share with teachers of Judaism of their time is based on the divine promise with which "the Law and the Prophets" concludes: "I will send the prophet Elijah to you before the coming of the awesome, fearful day of the LORD. He shall reconcile parents with children and children with their parents..." (Mal 3:23–24a; RSV: 4:5–6a). Concluding as it does "the Law and the Prophets," that is, the foundational part of the Hebrew Bible, the announcement of Elijah's return from the celestial sphere as harbinger of the onset of God's final intervention could not help but create the expectation to which Peter, James, and John refer.

1

Jesus' identification of John with the returned Elijah not only echoes Mk's introduction of the Baptist as clothed and girded like the man of Tishbe (comp. Mk 1:6 with 2 Kgs 1:8), but also locates the expected divine intervention in the time period that follows John's arrest. Now must be said what Jesus indeed proclaims, "The time is fulfilled and the Kingdom of God has come" (Mk 1:14–15). Now the divine acts unfold according to the scenario that the Tishbite's reappearance triggers. But what is its script? Does the manner of the narrative equation of John with Elijah provide a clue?

Indeed, several aspects of Mk's portrayal of the Baptist (Mk 1:2–11) direct the gospel's audience to 1 Kgs 17–2 Kgs 2, the section of the Hebrew Bible where Elijah's words and deeds are narrated. After preparing the readers for Elijah's appearance with two prooftexts, the first (Ex 23:20) from "the Law" and the second (Is 40:5) from "the Prophets," the gospel describes John's baptizing activity at the Jordan, the very place where in due time also Jesus, hailed by John as "a greater one than me, [who] comes after me," is baptized. And it is at that occasion that the man from Nazareth "saw the Heavens split (open) and the Spirit descending upon him like a dove." These features make the audience recall the narrative of Elijah's commissioning of Elisha as his successor and lead it to contemplate similar notions of the conveyance of the Spirit (2 Kgs 2:1–18).

Noteworthy as these correspondences are in their own right, they raise a far-reaching question: Does a similar correspondence exist between Elijah's successor Elisha and John's successor Jesus? Are also the conceptualization of Jesus and the narrative execution of the rest of the gospel shaped by a model, that is, the story of the man from Abel-meholah (1 Kgs 19:15–21, 2 Kgs 2:1–13:25)? To put it more broadly, is Mk's design of the LORD's expected intervention provided by the biblical story of the re-establishment of the LORD's reign in Samaria and Jerusalem through Elijah and Elisha (1 Kgs 17–2 Kgs 13)? In short, is the gospel of Mark composed according to a paradigm?

1.2 In Search of a Scenario

Since the investigation is not directly prompted by open questions in contemporary Markan research, it is guided by an exploratory logic that the introductory questions suggest and thus enters into debate with secondary literature only in the last chapters when the nature of Mark's hermeneutical activity is discussed. The study first presents and discusses the relevant evidence from the gospel itself, and by way of testing and conclusion seeks to relate the results of the investigation to several examples of Markan research. The outline is as follows.

After this introduction on the motivation for the search for a scenario of the Kingdom's manifestation (chapter 1), an exploration of a number of indicator passages seeks to make the case for the existence of a conceptual-narrative paradigm for the gospel and for its identification with the Elijah/Elisha Narrative (1 Kgs 17–2 Kgs 13) (chapter 2). The gospel's re-creation of the paradigm is then analyzed, from its plot and theme as a whole to the formal and thematic aspects of its narrative execution in detail, thus showing how the evangelist transforms the paradigm into a John/Jesus Story. We discuss first the scenario of the Kingdom's manifestation as the evangelist perceived it in the Elijah/Elisha Narrative (chapter 3), and then examine forms of narration employed by Mark (chapter 4) as well as narrative motifs and plots (chapters 5 and 6).

The unique features of the evangelist's compositional activity are then identified and reviewed (chapter 7) and its possible analogies in early Jewish and Roman-Hellenistic literature are explored (chapter 8). In the conclusion (chapter 9) the question of Mark's audience is raised and, after a look at some recent research, the evangelist's unique bid for biblical legitimation is discussed.

Chapter 2

The Case for a Paradigm

Several passages in Mk seem to suggest that a literary model provides formal and thematic features, the combination of which characterizes the gospel.

The following texts will be discussed in order to explore this possibility: (1) the people's response to Jesus' healing of the deaf-mute person (Mk 7:37), (2) Jesus' response to the question of by what authority he cleansed the Temple (Mk 11:29–30), (3) Jesus' affirmation after John's arrest that the time is fulfilled and the Kingdom has drawn near (Mk 1:14–15), (4) Jesus' statement, made with reference to the parable of the sower, that to his disciples, but not to "outsiders," the secret of the Kingdom has already been given (Mk 4:11), (5) the express identification of the gospel's first sentence as its "beginning" (Mk 1:1–3), (6) Jesus' question addressed to his disciples whether even after his second miraculous feeding of thousands they "still do not comprehend" (Mk 8:21), and (7) the narration of Peter's triple denial of his master (Mk 14:30, 72).

Our exploration will concentrate on textual aspects that, expressly or implicitly, point to a given scenario or employ a narrative motif according to which the divine intervention is conceptualized and told. And in light of the gospel's equation of John the Baptist with Elijah, already discussed, our investigation will relate the Markan texts to 1 Kgs 17–2 Kgs 13, seeking to determine whether and in what manner the latter provides a model for the former.

2.1 The Measure of Jesus' Deeds (Mk 7:37)

Jesus' healing of the deaf-mute person (Mk 7:31–37) is told immediately before the first narration of the doubling of a miracle, that of the feeding of thousands (Mk 8:1–9, comp. 6:35–44; for a second doubling comp. Mk 9:14–29 with 7:31–37, and below 4.3.1). Moreover, as at the beginning of the work (Mk 1:27), so also here the people respond to Jesus' act of power in amazement. However, now they go further and observe that "he has done all (things) well," concluding their statement with a proof-text from Is 35:5. To what does the noun "all" refer? And what does the adverb "well" mean in this context? These characterizations of Jesus' deeds evidently imply a quantitative and qualitative standard according to which his performance is measured. What is that criterion? How are its two aspects defined and employed?

a. We begin with an exploration of the numerically defined element. The people's observation — singular in Mk and without parallel in the other gospels — suggests that with this particular miracle Jesus' deeds of power have satisfied a numerically defined standard of completeness. Hence the question: How many miracle stories have by now been told? The following listing serializes them unit by literary unit (thus irrespective of the number of beneficiaries).

1. Jesus' exorcism of an unclean spirit: Mk 1:23–26

2. Jesus' healing of Peter's mother-in-law: Mk 1:29–31

3. Jesus' healing and exorcism of many in the evening: Mk 1:32–34

4. Jesus' cleansing of a leper: Mk 1:40–45

5. Jesus' healing of a paralytic man: Mk 2:1–12

6. Jesus' restoration of a withered hand: Mk 3:1-5

7. Jesus' healing and exorcism of many from many regions: Mk 3:7-12

8. Jesus' command to wind and water: Mk 4:35-41

9. Jesus' expulsion of Legion: Mk 5:1-20

10. Jesus' healing of the hemorrhaging woman and revival of Jairus' daughter: Mk 5:21-43

11. Jesus' healing of a few sick persons in Nazareth: Mk 6:5 (1-6)

12. Jesus' feeding of 5,000 men with five loaves and two fishes: Mk 6:32-44

13. Jesus' walking on the Sea of Galilee: Mk 6:45-52

14. Jesus' healing of many at the Sea of Galilee: Mk 6:53-56

15. Jesus' expulsion of an unclean spirit: Mk 7:24-30

16. Jesus' restoration of a deaf-mute person: Mk 7:31-37

The relatively high number of miracles itself directs readers to that figure in the Hebrew Scriptures who is credited with many deeds of power: Elisha. In the stories about him (2 Kgs 2:19–13:25), Gehazi's rehearsal of "all the great deeds which Elisha has done" (2 Kgs 8:4 [1–6]) not only serializes them but also indicates that their cumulation legitimates him as the prophet divinely empowered to re-establish the LORD's sovereignty in Samaria (as well as in Damascus and, indirectly, Jerusalem; 2 Kgs 8:7–12:17). But do they add up to sixteen? A serialization of Elisha's deeds of power may be made as follows:

1. Elisha's parting of the Jordan: 2 Kgs 2:13-15

2. Elisha's cure of the water of Jericho: 2 Kgs 2:19-22

3. Elisha's curse of the mocking children: 2 Kgs 2:23–24

4. Elisha's supply of water in the desert: 2 Kgs 3:4–20

5. Elisha's supply of oil for the widow's jar: 2 Kgs 4:1–7

6. Elisha's overcoming the Shunammite's childlessness: 2 Kgs 4:8–17

7. Elisha's revival of the Shunammite's son: 2 Kgs 4:18–37

8. Elisha's cure of the inedible stew: 2 Kgs 4:38–41

9. Elisha's feeding of the hundred with twenty loaves: 2 Kgs 4:42–44

10. Elisha's cleansing of Naaman's leprosy: 2 Kgs 5:1–19

11. Elisha's affliction of Gehazi with Naaman's leprosy: 2 Kgs 5:20–27

12. Elisha's raising of a submerged axe: 2 Kgs 6:1–7

13. Elisha's gift of sight to his servant: 2 Kgs 6:15b–17

14. Elisha's closing and opening of the Arameans' eyes: 2 Kgs 6:18–23

15. Elisha's foreknowledge of the end of the famine: 2 Kgs 6:24–7:20

16. The revival of a corpse that touched Elisha's bones: 2 Kgs 13:20–21

The correspondence between the sum total of Elisha's deeds and the number of Jesus' miracles up to Mk 7:37 can hardly be mere coincidence. On the other hand, the hypothesis that the Elisha Narrative is a conceptual and narrative paradigm for Mk is able to explain the appearance and significance of the quantitative aspect of Mk 7:37.

b. Jesus' deeds are also measured qualitatively in Mk 7:37:
They have been done "well." Are they in this respect, too,
compared to those of Elisha, and consequently described as more
powerful and beneficial than they? Two examples illustrate that
the answer is affirmative.

First, while Elisha feeds a hundred men with the help of
one servant, offering them twenty loaves (and some garden produce) and has all satisfied, Jesus feeds 5,000 men through the
services of twelve disciples, doing so with only five loaves (and
two fishes), and not only has them sated but also has twelve
baskets of leftovers collected. Here a fourfold heightening is observable: More people are fed, a larger number of servants are
used, more is left over, and fewer loaves are used. Jesus manifestly accomplishes a greater feat since he does so with fewer
loaves and sustains more people (2 Kgs 4:42–44 / Mk 6:32–44).

Second, when Elisha raises the Shunammite woman's son,
he locks himself into the upper room with the child's body and,
after prayer, positions his body on that of the child — mouth to
mouth, eyes on eyes, hands over hands — and thus brings the
child back to life. But when Jesus revives a child, he enters the
room where she lies, not alone but with her parents and three
disciples; he takes her hand, commands her to rise, and she
stands up. Thus to the detailed series of Elisha's actions done
in the privacy of the prophet's chamber there corresponds the
comparatively effortless and public activity of Jesus, climaxed in
a command. Jesus' revival of the child demonstrates that he is
more powerful than Elisha — evidently a qualitative heightening
of the scriptural model (2 Kgs 4:18–37/Mk 5:21–24 and Mk 35–
43).

In sum, the explanation of both the quantitative and the
qualitative aspects of the implied standard according to which
Jesus' miracles told in Mk 1:14–7:37 are measured suggests that
Jesus is portrayed as a greater Elisha.

We turn to another passage in Mk that assumes a logical
connection between Jesus' baptism by John, as narrated at the
beginning of the gospel, and a climax of his public activity in

the Temple cleansing — a connection for which 1 Kgs 17–2 Kgs 13 may supply the rationale.

2.2 The Authority of John's Baptism (Mk 11:29–30)

Toward the end of Jesus' public activity, when he visits the Temple in Jerusalem, the chief priests, theologians, and elders approach him and ask him in whose authority he acted when he cleansed the Temple, banishing certain mercantile enterprises (Mk 11:27–33, comp. 11:15–18). Jesus agrees to answer their query if they first respond to a counter-question: Is the baptism of John — with which he was initiated into his mission — of divine or human origin? The respondents fail to answer because both possible replies would embarrass them. Accordingly also Jesus remains silent and does not identify the source of his authority to purify the holy precinct. This leaves the readers without an answer as well. What is the logic of the connection between John's Baptism and Jesus' eventual cleansing of the Temple? A linkage is assumed, but of what nature is it?

A review of 2 Kgs 2–13 shows that the train of events set into motion by Elisha's commissioning by Elijah, located at the Jordan and sealed with the conveyance of a double portion of the Tishbite's spirit (2 Kgs 2:1–18), eventually led to the reestablishment of the LORD's sovereignty in Samaria and the Kingdom of Israel (2 Kgs 9:1–10:31) as well as in Jerusalem and the Kingdom of Judah (2 Kgs 11:1–12:17). In the latter location the victory over apostasy is eventually climaxed in King Joash's setting in order the affairs of the Temple (2 Kgs 12:5–17). In other words, the authorization for that action carried out within Jerusalem's sanctuary ultimately derives from the seminal act of Elijah's commissioning of Elisha.

In Mk 11:27–33 Jesus' question remains without answer. But the linkage of his commissioning by John to that of Elisha by Elijah implies a similar causal relation between the eventual Temple cleansing by Jesus and the ordering of the affairs of the LORD's house by Joash. That compositional feature of the

Elisha Narrative illuminates the logic of Jesus' counter-question
in Mk 11:29–30. We turn to a similar examination of Jesus'
first words of proclamation, affirming that with John's arrest
the time is fulfilled (Mk 1:14–15).

2.3   The Fullness of the Kingdom's Time (Mk 1:15)

What scenario of divine intervention does the gospel presup-
pose when it initiates Jesus' preaching with the words, "The
appointed time period is completed and the Kingdom of God
has drawn near. Change your mind and believe the good news!"
(Mk 1:15)? The introduction of this proclamation indicates that
Jesus begins his activity after John's arrest. Thus Jesus' baptism and the removal of his predecessor from the public sphere
trigger, as it were, Jesus' public activity. Does this periodization
correspond to a similar one in 1 Kgs 17–2 Kgs 13?

Elisha's public activity did not begin until Elijah had at the
Jordan conveyed his spirit to his successor (the latter's earlier
call to discipleship notwithstanding) and until the man from
Abel-meholah had witnessed his master taken from earth and
assumed into the celestial sphere (2 Kgs 2:1–18, comp. 1 Kgs
19:19–21 and 2 Kgs 2:19–8:6). In accord with this sequence the
public activity of Mark's Jesus does not begin until John had
at the Jordan commissioned the man from Nazareth and then
himself been taken away from the terrestrial realm (Mk 1:9–11,
15a, comp. 6:14–29, 9:11–13). By the same token, Elisha's activity, once he had been commissioned, gradually makes manifest
the LORD's sovereignty among the people at large and, in due
time, leads to its full establishment (comp. 2 Kgs 2:19–8:6 with
8:7–10:28/13:1–25 and 11:1–12:17).

If this correspondence is assumed, several aspects of the
opening proclamation of Jesus appear in a new light. (1) The
reference to the completion of the appointed timespan alludes
to the period of Elijah's activity (1 Kgs 17–2 Kgs 1), summarily seen as a period of preparation that draws to its close with
Elijah's assumption and Elisha's commissioning at the Jordan

(2 Kgs 2:1–18). (2) When Mark's Jesus speaks of the arrival of the divine rule, it is portrayed according to its scriptural timing: As Elisha's traversing the land doing good gradually manifests the LORD's sovereignty, so Jesus' words and deeds show the growing presence of God's rule. (3) By the same token, the call to "change one's mind" and "to believe in the good news" is the invitation to accept the scriptural paradigm of divine intervention that the gospel presents and to set aside other models of expectation. (4) Finally, Mark's identification of Jesus' preaching as "the good news" (commonly rendered "the gospel") echoes its use in 2 Kgs 7:3–13. There the discovery by four lepers of the miraculous lifting of an almost successful Aramean siege of Israel's capital becomes the announcement of "good news" to the royal house and the city (2 Kgs 7:9).

In sum, the beginning of Jesus' public activity corresponds to that of Elisha in a manner similar to the way in which the completion of Jesus' sixteen miracles in Mk 1:14–7:37 correlates to the sum total of those accomplished by Elisha. This suggests a question: Is the entire scenario of the Kingdom's establishment, into which the various correspondences would fit, a subject of discussion in Mk? We turn to an investigation of Mk's master parable, that of the sower (Mk 4:3–20).

2.4 The Parable of the Kingdom's Secret (Mk 4:11)

The parable of the sower (Mk 4:3–20) details three kinds of failure as well as three numerically graduated kinds of success. When the disciples ask Jesus about this procedure of teaching, he not only affirms that they have already been given "the secret of the Kingdom of God," but also expresses surprise that they don't know the solution of this parable. Then, before he proceeds to offer what they ask, he identifies this parable as the key to the others: "If you do not know (the solution of) this parable, how will you then know all the (other) parables?" If it is the master parable, does it refer in a comprehensive manner to the scenario of the Kingdom's coming — or, since its secret

is already known to the disciples, to aspects of its coming that
need to be illuminated also for those who already know?

Jesus' solution constructs analogies between the act of sowing and that of setting forth "the word" (of the Kingdom), on
the one hand, and the seeds' failures and successes in bringing
fruit, on the other. Disciples as well as audience cannot but
think of the proclamation of the gospel and of the negative and
positive responses they witness — in fact, the narration of Mk to
a large extent serves to illustrate different kinds and degrees of
rejection or acceptance of Jesus' claims. A second look, however,
makes readers wonder whether Jesus' solutions of the negative
results do not make better sense than the features of the parable
as first told — what farmer would waste seed corn on a road surface or shallow soil? Moreover, why are the numerically defined
degrees of yield not explained? In short, is a constraint at work
in the formulation of both parable and solution?

The repetition of the series of three numerically defined degrees of success draws attention, especially since in both parable
and solution they come, climax-like, at the end. That the number "100" symbolizes the most completely positive response is,
even considering lower actual yields at that time and place, not
necessarily surprising. On the other hand, the gospel's express
equation of John the Baptist with Elijah and the — so far implicit — one of Jesus (in Mk 1:14-7:37) with Elisha, shows that
the Elijah/Elisha Narrative in a unique way defines the expectation horizon of "those who have ears to hear." And it is in that
sustained biblical story that the numerical value "100" twice
appears as indicator of the result of a person's complete obedience to the divine word. There is Ahab's chamberlain Obadiah
whose faithfulness to the LORD makes him hide "a hundred
men of the LORD's prophets" who thus escaped Jezebel's mas-
sacre (2 Kgs 18:13). By the same token, Elijah successfully
calls down fire on two groups of fifty men, sent by the apostate
Ahaziah to arrest him (2 Kgs 1:9-12). Is the choice of the number "100" in Mk 4:1-20 informed by its use in the Elijah/Elisha
Narrative?

Alerted by this correspondence, readers think of further connections. The three kinds of negative response — from immediate rejection through only short-lived acceptance to rejection eventually caused by worldly pressures — find fitting illustrations in Jezebel's outright opposition to Elijah (1 Kgs 19:1-2), Ahab's temporary obedience (1 Kgs 18:41-46/21:1-22:40), and the Israelite King Jehoram's first positive, but eventually negative response to prophetic words (2 Kgs 3:2, 10-27, 6:24-33, 9:21-26). On the other hand, the formal — and in biblical literature rare — feature of parable narration followed by the express supply of a solution, appears once each in Mk (4:3-9/13-20) and in the Elijah/Elisha Narrative (1 Kgs 20:35-40/41-42).

In short, the parable of the sower seems to use the plot of 1 Kgs 17-2 Kgs 13 as conceptual-narrative foil for its description of the responses to be expected in relation to Jesus' mission. And since it is pointedly identified as key to "all the parables," one wonders whether those that follow in Mk 4:21-32 do not highlight other aspects of the Elijah/Elisha Narrative that offer the key to certain features of the coming of the Kingdom through John and Jesus.

This is indeed the case. The four brief parables appear narratively well motivated if they are taken as highlighting in different ways a contrast between the inception and the completion of the sequence of events that establishes the LORD's sovereignty. (1) There is the small, seed-like beginning and the encompassing ending as pictured in the parable of the mustard seed (Mk 4:30-32), comparable to the progress from the first appearances of Elijah and Elisha to the eventual establishment of the LORD's rule in Aram, Israel, and Judah. (2) There is the orderly, graduated process of seed grains being planted, then sprouting, showing ears, and eventually bringing fruit calling forth the sickle, illustrating nature's power to move from sowing to harvest by itself (Mk 4:26-29), comparable to the unimpedible process with which the first, seemingly insignificant demonstrations of the LORD's power in Elijah's and Elisha's deeds lead, stage by stage, to a harvest that establishes the divine rule in

capital and kingdom. (3) Mk 4:24–25, through the context identified as a parabolic saying, affirms the principle "measure for
measure, and then some" — both for those who have and those
who do not. The principle is starkly illustrated by the way in
which Jezebel, who slaughters the LORD's prophets, soon finds
her Baal prophets killed (1 Kgs 18:13/40), not to mention her
own infamous end (2 Kgs 9:30–37)! (4) Finally, the parabolic
saying concerning lamp and bushel leads to the affirmation that
whatever is hidden will become visible (Mk 4:21–22). Does it refer to what happened with the news of the LORD's defeat of the
Aramean siege army, unknown to king and people of Samaria
but discovered at night by the four lepers and quickly announced
and publicly confirmed in daylight (2 Kgs 7:3–15)?

The correspondences, taken together, confirm the claim of
Mark's Jesus that once the solution of the master parable is
understood, the other parables are also explained. If the manner of the establishment of the LORD's rule as plotted in 1 Kgs
17–2 Kgs 13 is Mk's paradigm (subject to transformation by
heightening and expansion), then the parables of Mk 4:1–34 focus on various aspects of the model story in order to show that
these characterize also the course and reception of the present
establishment of God's sovereignty. Is that also true of Mk's
beginning point in plot, time, and space? We turn to a consid-
eration of its opening line.

2.5   The Identification of the Gospel's Beginning (Mk 1:1–3)

It is unusual to begin a composition with the identification of its
opening as its "beginning." Is this not self-evident? Moreover,
while all the canonical gospels end with the double theme of
Jesus' martyrdom and assumption, they differ markedly in their
beginnings. Are these differences and Mk's formulation due to
compositional constraints?

As for Mk, this seems indeed to be the case. The first major
section of its scriptural model is devoted to Elijah as precursor

of Elisha (1 Kgs 17–2 Kgs 2). Given the express identification of the Baptist with the man from Tishbe, Mk's work can only begin where it does: with the appearance of John, and that "in the wilderness" and as one who is active at the Jordan. Its identification as the gospel's beginning thus becomes intelligible. Hence the further question: Does Mk's disposition offer additional structuring indicators?

We turn to a discussion of Jesus' feeding of 4,000, the first miracle after he has completed the sixteen deeds of power that show him as measuring up to the standards set by Elisha.

2.6 The Doubling of the Miraculous Feeding (Mk 8:21)

After the healing of the deaf-mute person (Mk 7:31–37) has made Jesus' miracles equal in number and superior in kind to Elisha's sixteen, the feeding of 4,000 is told (Mk 8:1–9). It is in motif and narration a doubling of the feeding of 5,000 (Mk 6:32–44). The following exchanges with the disciples (Mk 8:14–21) show how crucial the seventeenth miracle is for the comprehension of what Jesus brings: If already the first feeding should have led the disciples to understand, how much more the second (comp. Mk 8:21 with 6:52)!

In 1 Kgs 17–2 Kgs 13 several of Elijah's deeds of power are duplicated by Elisha: Both supply sustenance to a faithful woman in need (1 Kgs 17:8–16/2 Kgs 4:1–7), revive the child of a woman who hosts them (1 Kgs 17:17–24/2 Kgs 4:18–37), and both prove superior when challenged by a hostile king (1 Kgs 18:16–38/2 Kgs 6:24–7:20). Moreover, postbiblical storytelling can affirm that Elisha's power exceeds that of Elijah because, in the words of Ginzberg, the former's "crossing of the Jordan . . . was more remarkable than the corresponding wonder done by Elijah, for Elisha traversed the river alone, and Elijah had been accompanied by Elisha" (IV 239). In the same vein storytellers can observe (again in Ginzberg's words) that "the promise made to Elisha by Elijah to give him 'a double por-

tion of his spirit'...was fulfilled; the master resuscitated only
one person, and the disciple two" (VI 347). Hence in comparison to Elisha's sixteen miracles "eight was all his master had
performed" (IV 239).

Thus, with the second feeding of thousands the miracles of
Mark's Jesus go in number beyond those of Elisha. Hence the
question: Does Jesus both measure up to and go beyond Elisha
in a manner comparable to the way in which Elisha exceeded
Elijah? Put differently: Does the gospel heighten the paradigm
in as far as the quantity of powerful deeds is concerned? The
answer is in the affirmative: Mk's narration of Jesus' feeding
5,000 heightens the motif of Elisha's supplying 100 (2 Kgs 4:42–
44), which, in turn, heightens the same motif found in Elijah's
feeding one needy person (1 Kgs 17:8–16). Furthermore, Mk's
emphasized doubling of the motif of feeding thousands adds a
further act to the plot of its biblical model.

Jesus' deeds of power narrated after Mk 7:37 add up to another eight. The following listing suggests itself:

17. Jesus' feeding of 4,000: Mk 8:1–9

18. Jesus' gift of sight to the blind man from Bethsaida: Mk
    8:22–26

19. Jesus' exorcism of the mute spirit: Mk 9:14–29

20. Jesus' gift of sight to blind Bartimaeus: Mk 10:46–52

21. Jesus' curse of the fig tree: Mk 11:12–14, 20–25

22. Jesus' cleansing of the Temple: Mk 11:15–17, 27–33

23. Jesus' death causing the Temple curtain to tear: Mk
    15:38

24. Jesus' rising from the tomb: Mk 16:1–8

As Elisha extends by eight Elijah's eight miracles, so now Jesus extends by another eight Elisha's sixteen. It is interesting

that Jesus does not double the number of Elisha's miracles; direct continuity with the scriptural model is sought, and in this manner Jesus' mission is conceptualized and legitimated.

We now turn to an exploration of the narration of Peter's denial (Mk 14:30) in order to probe the nature of the relation of Markan texts to 1 Kgs 17–2 Kgs 13 in the part of the gospel that follows Mk 7:37.

2.7 The Tripling of Peter's Denial (Mk 14:30, 72)

One of the memorable features of the Passion Story is Peter's denial of his master (Mk 14:26–31, 66–72). Why does the negative motif appear, and not once but three times? Moreover, why is it unfolded by employing the numerical sequence 2/3: "Before the cock crows twice, you will deny me thrice" (Mk 14:30, comp. 14:72)? Is a constraint at work that calls for the use of this constellation?

Peter's triple denial in the high priest's courtyard calls to mind, at least for readers who are alert to the mysterious presence of the Elijah/Elisha Narrative in the gospel, the narration of Elijah's last journey, on which his servant and disciple Elisha accompanies him (2 Kgs 2:1–12). Three times Elijah asks Elisha to stay behind and three times the latter responds, "I swear by the LORD's life and by your life that I will certainly not desert you!" He does know what also the members of the prophetic communities at Bethel and Jericho point out to him, namely, that on this day "the LORD takes your master away from your head." Elisha's triple affirmation of loyalty to his master to the very end is eventually rewarded with two portions of his master's spirit, thus making him the full successor of Elijah (comp. Dt 21:17). Hence, Elisha's triple affirmation of faithfulness, at the time when his master draws close to his departure from the terrestrial sphere, contrasts with the triple denial of Jesus by Peter, the spokesman among the disciples. More, he is pointedly shown to be unlike Elisha and hence not the kind of successor of Jesus that Elisha was in relation to Elijah. By the same token, this portrayal of Peter reinforces Mk's literary casting of John and Jesus as forerunner-successor pair of the order of Elijah and Elisha.

The numerical sequence 2/3 in Mk's Peter story is not only formally an inversion of the sequence 3/2 in 2 Kgs 2:1–18; it also echoes the juxtaposition of the two numbers in a story elsewhere in the Elijah/Elisha Story. In the narration of Jehu's overthrow of Jezebel, Sidonian princess by birth and prominent member of the Omride dynasty (2 Kgs 9:30–37), the usurper is sarcastically greeted by the queen when he enters the royal summer residence. Without ado he orders "two, three" courtiers who are close to her to throw her down. They comply and so Jezebel meets her death, betrayed by those whose office demands that they remain loyal to her. The numerical sequence 2/3 appears as another link between the gospel's narration and its biblical model. The apparent artificiality of Mk's employment of the two numbers is due to this narrative-conceptual constraint. In sum, in the part of Mk in which the plot development of divine intervention goes beyond that of the Elijah/Elisha Story, narrative motifs of the paradigm are also present.

2.8 Conclusion: Convergence Toward a Hypothesis

Each of the seven passages either implies or alludes to a scenario of divine intervention according to which the appearance of Jesus is conceptualized and told. To be sure, the disciples already know the plot and the major figures of the cast of the coming of the LORD's rule; it is "the secret of the Kingdom of God" and as such hidden from "outsiders." Does the gospel wish those who are not enlightened — including its audiences then and now — to engage in the search for that secret? If so, the inductive approach adopted above commends itself, all the more so because it seems to open the path to the unveiling of the secret.

Indeed, a close reading of the seven texts allows a composite though fragmentary description of that scenario and thus the tentative identification of a model. It is the story of the establishment of the LORD's rule in Aram, Israel, and Judah through divinely appointed men, notably the forerunner-successor pair Elijah-Elisha (1 Kgs 17–2 Kgs 13). Whether it is the gospel's point of narrative departure (Mk 1:1) or its extension of the scriptural paradigm (Mk 8:21), the logical connection between sequences of narrated events (Mk 1:15, 11:29–30) or its parabolic encoding (Mk 4:11), whether it is a numerical correspondence in plot development (Mk 7:37) or in narrative execution (Mk 14:30), the indicator passages converge in that they point to the Elijah/Elisha Narrative as a conceptual and narrative model for Mk.

The following chapters are devoted to the testing of the hypothesis. It is, to be sure, of a peculiar nature because it requires readers to enter a hermeneutic circle of its own: they are asked to look at Mk in the light of the Elijah/Elisha Narrative and, by the same token, read the latter with the eyes of the former. The interpretations thus define each other, and Mk makes the enterprise pointedly a journey of discovery by speaking of the secret of the Kingdom — without ever unveiling it! Thus the secrecy motif awakens the readers' curiosity and draws them into the search for the implied model and its presence in the gospel. This also means that different modes of interpretation are not applicable and have to be set aside because the testing of the hypothesis makes the hermeneutic circle "(Mark's) John/Jesus Narrative — Elijah/Elisha Narrative — John/Jesus Narrative" by necessity an exclusive one. In other words, 1 Kgs 17–2 Kgs 13 is read and appropriated only as it is read and appropriated by the second evangelist.

In the concluding chapters we will draw on other relevant literature, primary and secondary, that shows that Mk's relation to 1 Kgs 17–2 Kgs 13 does not exclude the identification of the presence of other shaping forces. The gospel may be expected to be heir to more than one legacy! It is the task of chapters 2–6 of this investigation to probe into Mk's relation to one of these legacies, that is, the one that the Hebrew Bible contains.

It succeeds to the extent to which it is able to demonstrate a unique connection between the Hebrew Scriptures, or a certain section of them, and the narrative conceptualization of Jesus' appearance that the second gospel presents.

The indicator passages just discussed suggest that the relationship has formal as well as thematic aspects, both of which may be perceived on two levels: that of the gospel in its entirety and that of its individual narrative units. Thus the gospel as a whole corresponds both structurally and materially in a significant manner to plot and theme of the Elijah/Elisha Narrative, and many of Mk's motifs and individual units correlate with their counterparts in one way formally and in another manner thematically. Hence a division of the analysis into several parts commends itself: Literary structure and master theme of the gospel as a whole (chapter 3), the forms of narration of its individual story units (chapter 4), and finally the discussion of a number of narrative motifs and plots (chapters 5 and 6).

Chapter 3

The Scenario of
the Kingdom's Coming

This chapter first explores how the evangelist weaves into the work cross references that suggest unity of conception (3.1). Then its formal structure as well as the spatial and temporal staging of its plot, in as far as they adopt and extend those of the model, claim our attention (3.2), followed by an excursus that shows that Mk's plot presentation agrees with that attributed to Peter in Acts 10:37–41 (3.3).

3.1 Literary Cross References

A casual reading of the gospel makes readers aware of its literary coherence because several passages speak of what is told later or earlier. A well known example is Jesus' triple announcement of his future martyrdom and resurrection, which the last part of the work narrates (comp. Mk 8:31, 9:31, and 10:33–34 with 14:1–16:8). These predictions and their fulfilment span the second half of the gospel. However, already at its beginning the evangelist has both Jesus and his opponents refer to his death (comp. Mk 2:20 and 3:6 with 11:18, on the one hand, and with 10:45 and 14:1–15:39, on the other). Shorter spans of texts also are bracketed by an anticipation-realization schema, notably prediction and narration of Peter's triple denial (comp. Mk 14:29–31 with 14:66–72), first and second reference to the disciples' continued failure to comprehend the significance of Jesus' miraculous feedings of thousands (comp. Mk 8:21 with 6:52), and Jesus' reference to John's baptism when challenged in relation to his cleansing of the Temple (comp. Mk 11:29–30 with 1:4, 9–11).

Mk's reading of 1 Kgs 17–2 Kgs 13 evidently perceived a direct, causal connection between Elisha's commissioning by Elijah (2 Kgs 2:1–18) and King Joash's ordering of the affairs of the Jerusalem Temple told as the last act of the establishment of the LORD's rule (2 Kgs 12:5–17): The latter is ultimately triggered — hence legitimated — by the former. Those who recognize this relationship thus also know how to answer Jesus' counter-question addressed to those who enquire into his authority to cleanse the Temple (Mk 11:27–33, comp. 11:15–18 and 2.2 above). The example shows that Mk read 1 Kgs 17– 2 Kgs 13 as an internally coherent composition and thus could use suitable elements of its narrative execution to establish a claim on behalf of Jesus (see 2.1, 2.3, and 2.4. for further examples).

There is little doubt that the Elijah/Elisha Narrative impresses readers as a sustained story in its own right. It is not only set off from what precedes and follows through the front-stage action of Elijah and Elisha, whose lively tales of charismatic words and deeds contrast with the chronicle-like narration that frames 1 Kgs 17–2 Kgs 13, but it is also internally bound together through cross references. This may be illustrated with several examples.

When the king of Israel requests that Elisha's servant Gehazi tell him about his master, he does so with the words: "Do recount to me all the great things which Elisha has done" (2 Kgs 8:4). The continuation in 8:4–6 shows that Elisha's deeds of power collected in 2 Kgs 2:13–7:20 are Gehazi's topic. Hence that series of short and longer stories, together with its introduction in 2 Kgs 2:1–12, presents itself as a coherent literary unit. Moreover, the connection of Elisha with Elijah made in 1 Kgs 19:15–17 connects the call of the man from Abel-meholah to become prophet in Elijah's place with the parallel divine calls of Hazael and Jehu as kings-to-be (2 Kgs 8:7–15, 8:28–10:28). The Joash story (2 Kgs 11:1–12:22), on the other hand, is prepared by and related to the Hazael/Jehu narration by the brief story of Jehu's extermination of forty-two members of the Davidic royal house when they were on the road to Jezreel in order to visit their sick relative (2 Kgs 8:28–29/10:13–14). Their slaughter prompts Queen Athaliah's murder of those still alive of the royal house in Jerusalem and hence leads to the chain of events that brought her overthrow and death, the elimination of Baalism in Jerusalem, the enthronement of the seven-year-old Joash, the renewal of the covenant, and the ordering of the affairs of the Temple (2 Kgs 11:1–12:20). Finally, the narratives relating to Elisha's last days (2 Kgs 13:1, 10–25) are through an ominous outcry connected to that story that, hinge-like, already connects the Elijah and the Elisha stories: "My Father! My Father! Horses of Israel and its horsemen!" (comp. 2 Kgs 13:14 with 2:12–13).

To conclude, while internal cross referencing characterizes 1 Kgs 17–2 Kgs 13, it cannot be argued that there is a unique compositional correspondence between it and Mk. It does, however, provide a first and readily perceived signal that a composition seeks to present itself as a coherent unit, thus inviting the audience to identify and ponder more specific indicators of the work's literary-conceptual thrust.

3.2   Structure and Theme

Mk recognized not only coherent narrative progress in 1 Kgs 17–2 Kgs 13 but also a plot made up of several acts and supported by staging in space and time. This is illustrated by the gospel's use of the story of Elisha's commissioning by Elijah (2 Kgs 2:1–18), seen as end of a first as well as beginning of a second act. The passing of the action from legitimating forerunner to greater

successor underlies Jesus' opening statement that "the time is
fulfilled" (Mk 1:15): The period allotted to the activity of John
as returned Elijah comes to its end once the Baptist is removed
from the public stage and Jesus, Elisha's counterpart, begins to
set in motion the train of events that leads to the establishment
of God's rule. On the other hand, once Jesus has performed
sixteen miracles, the standard set by Elisha, the next act of the
plot can begin, leading to the fateful confrontations in the capitals (comp. 2.1 and 2.6 above). It seems that the (exclusively
Markan) parable of the seed growing by itself (Mk 4:26–29) reflects four successive stages of the Kingdom's establishment by
portraying the progress of the seed's unimpedible growth (see
2.4 above).

In sum, four acts may be identified and abstracted in this
way: (1) The words and deeds of Elijah, the desert-born man
of God, lead to the divinely confirmed commission of a greater
prophetic successor, Elisha of Abel-meholah, who will eventually
bring about the overthrow of apostasy in capital and kingdom
(1 Kgs 17:1–2 Kgs 2:12). (2) Elisha's deeds and words, through
which he publicly vindicates himself as the divinely empowered
agent of the LORD's presence (2 Kgs 2:1–8:6), lead to (3) the initiation and execution of the overthrow of the apostasy of Baalism in the capitals and kingdoms of Aram, Israel, and Judah
(2 Kgs 8:7–15/8:16–10:28/11:1–16, 18a). (4) The brief portrayal
of the continuance of the new state of affairs, that is, the LORD's
sovereignty and the rule of his royal and cultic agents in Israel
and Judah (2 Kgs 10:29–32/11:17, 18b–22/13:1–25), concludes
the plot.

3.2.1 The Four Acts

Several of the indicator passages suggest that the gospel's narration moves through distinct acts. The commissioning of Jesus
by John at the Jordan concludes the first, brief section and initiates Jesus' public activity in word and deed, recognized as "a
new teaching in power" (Mk 1:27). Halfway through the gospel

the people's response with which Jesus' sixteenth miracle story
ends (Mk 7:37) implies that the climax that has been reached
also opens a further act of the plot, that of the final, decisive
confrontation. Finally, while Jesus' martyrdom is the result of
the conflict, it is not the last word: the gospel ends with the
affirmation that he is risen (Mk 16:6). Thus four acts may be
identified:

1. The Commissioning of the Kingdom's Bringer:
   Mk 1:1–13

2. The Authentication of the Kingdom's Bringer:
   Mk 1:14–7:37

3. The Confrontation with the Powers of Apostasy:
   Mk 8:1–15:39

4. The Vindication of the Bringer of the Kingdom:
   Mk 15:40–16:8

The outline corresponds to that of the Elijah/Elisha Narrative
in that both move through four acts, both present a forerunner-
successor pair as the main actors, and both stage the action as
moving from the Jordan through the countryside of both the
Land of Canaan and regions of its neighbors to the center of
royal apostasy, where the conflict comes to a head and beyond
which the overthrow of apostasy makes its impact. Most of all,
the theme of the plot is the same: The re-establishment of the
rule of the LORD, the God of Israel, among those who claim
descent from Jacob-Israel.

Two obvious differences must be noted. Mk's first part (Mk
1:1–13) is in narrative execution considerably shorter than its
counterpart (1 Kgs 17:1–2 Kgs 1:18), concentrating as it does on
John's commissioning of the man from Nazareth and the context information needed. Then, Mk's third part (Mk 8:1–15:39)
portrays the establishment of divine rule as achieved through
the martyrdom and death of the Kingdom's bringer while the

corresponding part of the Elijah/Elisha Narrative (2 Kgs 8:7–12:22) tells of the establishment through the preservation and continuing life of Jehu and Joash, its two royal agents. These divergences reflect constraints with which the evangelist began: the death of Jesus on a Roman cross and, probably, the known competition of the movement of John with that of Jesus (see Acts 19:1–7). Formally, however, the four parts of Mk correspond to those of 1 Kgs 17–2 Kgs 13.

3.2.2 Spatial and Temporal Staging

The gospel's spatial staging accords with that of the scripturally given plot. The action moves from the fringe of the Transjordanian desert, Elijah's home, to the Jordan, the traditional point of entry into the land of promise (1 Kgs 17:1–2 Kgs 2:18). From there Elisha's journeys take him to Jericho, then to the Jordan valley, the Jezreel plain, the Ephraimite hills, and finally to Samaria, the capital (2 Kgs 2:19–8:6). He encounters Israel's neighbors as well (2 Kgs 3:1–27, 5:1–19, 6:8–23, 6:24–7:20, comp. 8:1–6). The decisive confrontations in which Elisha is directly or indirectly involved take place in the urban-royal centers, near Damascus, Jezreel, Samaria, and Jerusalem (2 Kgs 8:7–12:17). And it is from there that the LORD's royal and prophetic servants eventually make effective the LORD's sovereignty (esp. 13:1–25).

The temporal staging of 1 Kgs 17–2 Kgs 13 is fitted into the chronological framework of its wider context, the Former Prophets (see the chronicling paragraphs throughout that larger work). Thus the encounters of Elijah and Micaiah, son of Imlah, with Israelite kings relate to the second and third monarchs of the Omride dynasty, Ahab and Ahaziah (1 Kgs 17:1–22:40; 1 Kgs 22:52–2 Kgs 1:18), while those of Elisha concern the last ruler of that house, Joram (2 Kgs 3:1–8:6, comp. 9:16–26). Jezebel's activity spans the times of both Elijah and Elisha (1 Kgs 18:4 ... 2 Kgs 9:30–37). The time that elapses from Elijah's commissioning of Elisha to the designation of Jehu through a servant of the latter is a span of at least eleven years (2 Kgs 2:1–18, 3:1–3, 8:16–24, 25–27, 9:29); another seven years pass until Athaliah's rule is overthrown (2 Kgs 9:28–29, 10:12–14, 11:1–16). On the other hand, Ahab's repentance after the murder of Naboth delays the announced destruction of his dynasty by one generation (1 Kgs 21:27–29), thus introducing a retarding element. Finally, though Elisha had been called to become the Tishbite's servant-disciple well before the latter's assumption (1 Kgs 19:15–17, 19–21), Elisha's public activity begins only after his predecessor's departure from earth (2 Kgs 2:13–15), thus stressing the notion of a unilinear succession in both time and space.

3.3 Excursus: Peter's Preaching according to Acts

Luke presents in Acts 10:37–41 an abstract of Peter's preaching. The occasion is the conversion of the Roman official Cornelius to Christ, and that of Peter to the insight that God is no respecter of persons because those acceptable to God are found both among Judeans and non-Judeans, those who observe the Law and those who do not (Acts 10:34–35). Thus a barrier between Peter's people and the rest of Noah's and Abraham's descendants has been overcome and peace has been established between them. Luke's summary of the apostle's preaching is characterized by the same division into four acts that is apparent in Mk:

1. It began, after the baptism that John preached in Galilee, with Jesus who came from Nazareth, whom God anointed with the holy spirit and with power (Acts 10:37b–38a, comp. Mk 1:1–13).

2. He went through the land doing good deeds and healing all who were possessed by the devil, because God was with him (Acts 10:38b, comp. Mk 1:14–7:37).

3. We have witnessed all his actions in the land of the Jews and in Jerusalem. And this man they put to death, having fastened him to wood (Acts 10:39, comp. Mk 8:1–15:39).

4. This man God raised on the third day and let him appear not to all the people but only to us witnesses predestined by God, who ate and drank with him after his rising from the dead (Acts 10:40–41, comp. Mk 15:40–16:8[20]).

This outline of Peter's preaching not only corresponds to that of Mk but also is pointedly differentiated from that of Paul, summarized in Acts 13:16–41 and evidently based on a different hermeneutic of the Scriptures. In short, the Lukan portrayal of Peter's preaching confirms our characterization of that presented by Mk, and the characteristic plot of the latter corresponds, in turn, to that of the Elijah/Elisha Narrative.

Chapter 4

Forms of Narration

Three formal aspects, each found both in Mk and 1 Kgs 17–2 Kgs 13, may be distinguished: (1) the relation of individual scene stories to each other and to the narration of the gospel as a whole; (2) the characteristic features of the scene stories, such as "parables," allowing the construction of a typology; and (3) the various manners of their connection with each other for the sake of certain narrative effects, such as doubling (see 2.6 above).

4.1 Independent and Subordinate Scene Stories

Viewed in its entirety, the narration of the gospel is made up of smaller units that, chainlike, are set into a sequence. The manner in which Mk is constituted by many scenes is evident not only in the brief first and last parts, which respectively move to Jesus' baptism and resurrection as climax (Mk 1:1–13, 15:40–16:8[20]), but especially in the two long parts that together constitute most of the gospel's volume. Thus in the third part (Mk 8:1–15:39) a sustained succession of scenes begins, after the doubling of the miraculous feeding and the two-staged gift of sight to the blind man (Mk 8:1–21, 22–26) have signalled its inception, with Jesus' three-staged announcement of future martyrdom. It then moves through various words and deeds demonstrating his authority and comes to its climax in a scene-by-scene narration of the confrontation in Jerusalem, manifest in Jesus' suffering and death. Here each scene is based on the preceding one and is, in turn, the preparation for the following one; only in as far as each is read in this context is it properly understood. On the other hand, this is not the case in the second part (Mk 1:14–7:37). Here the individual scenes are by and large independent of each other and do not need to be read in the light of the context, notwithstanding the observations that we have already made concerning Mk 7:37, one of the indicator passages (see 2.1 above), that the implied serialization of the stories of Jesus' miracles up to that point in the narrative is significant.

This compositional difference is found in the Elijah/Elisha Narrative as well. Its third part (2 Kgs 8:7–12:22; comp. 1 Kgs 19:15–18) is a sustained and literarily unified narration of the confrontations with apostasy, while the preceding second part (2 Kgs 2:1–8:6) is made up of individual text units that are coherent within themselves and independent of each other. In short, the transition from a series of independent, brief scenes to a logically progressing, sustained narration that subordinates to itself smaller units, appears in both Mk and its model, and that approximately at midpoint.

4.2   Types of Scenes

A grouping of the scenes by literary type is suggested by the gospel itself when it identifies several of them, found scattered throughout the work, as "parables": Mk 3:23–27, 4:1–34, 7:1–23, and 12:2–11. Apart from the general identification of what Jesus presents as "teaching" (Mk 1:22, 27; 4:1, 2) no specific names are given for other forms into which his teaching is cast, but in light of the Elijah/Elisha Narrative three other types may be identified: dialog narratives, vision/audition stories, and action episodes. The first two share with Mk's parable type what seems to be a central element in all forms, that of an exchange that leads to an insight and thus conveys a teaching; the scene units constructed according to these types make up most of the gospel. The correspondence of types between Mk and its scriptural paradigm calls for a fuller discussion.

4.2.1 Parabolic Compositions

Jesus repeatedly presents what he identifies as "parables" (e.g., Mk 4:1, 2, 33, 34) and affirms that the key to all of them is the parable of the sower (Mk 4:3–20). As master parable it veils for outsiders what the disciples as insiders already know: the secret of the Kingdom (Mk 4:11; see 2.4 above). To judge by this example, the parabler proceeds by constructing an everyday story in such a manner that several of its traits might be discovered to correspond to aspects of a certain (narrated) occurrence that the parabler wishes to be understood more deeply or differently. Then the detection of the correlation is through a clue left to the hearers who, if they successfully meet the challenge, come through their own effort to the deeper insight. In Mk's lead parable Jesus supplies, in response to the disciples' expression of uncertainty about the deeper insight to be conveyed, a clue in the form of equations of the seed with the divine word and of degrees of the seed's failure or success with the various human responses to that word. The solution that he thus in fact gives explains human rejection and reception of "the word" offered through Jesus and the disciples. Does not the Elijah/Elisha Narrative portray that range from outright repudiation to complete obedience in relation to the divine summons conveyed through prophets?

It is noteworthy that 1 Kgs 17–2 Kgs 13 also contains a parabolic composition together with its solution. It is the symbolic action of an unnamed prophet, disguised as soldier, who requests King Ahab to settle a (fictitious) law case. As soon as the king has pronounced the predictable verdict, the prophet removes the bandage that disguised his prophetic identity and thus prompts the monarch to realize that the law case is in fact

a parable. The prophet then proceeds to solve it by showing
that the king's mild treatment of the defeated Aramean king
amounts to disobedience to the divine command and thus calls
forth the LORD's displeasure (1 Kgs 20:35–43). Mk's parable
of the sower corresponds formally to this text not only in the
paralleling of the traits of the symbolic story itself, but also in
the addition of a "solution." The latter appears both in Mk and
in 1 Kgs 17–2 Kgs 13 only once.

Beyond this formal correspondence in parable construction
Mk's readers recognize in the parable of the disobedient vineyard keepers (Mk 12:2–12) both thematic and allegorical correlations with the only vineyard story in 1 Kgs 17–2 Kgs 13: the
Naboth Narrative (1 Kgs 21:1–29; for its role in the portrayal
of Jesus' martyrdom, see 6.2.3 below).

4.2.2 Dialog Narratives

Many of Mk's units quote, directly or indirectly, exchanges between Jesus and his partners. Unless such a text unit is expressly identified as parable or is a vision-audition story because
it makes the interaction between the terrestrial and the celestial
spheres a constituent formal element, it may be categorized as
a dialog narrative. Its narrative frame may be minimal, as in
Jesus' rebuttal of the claim of Davidic descent for the Anointed
One (Mk 12:35–37), or extensive by providing a narration of a
series of actions that motivate several exchanges, as in the story
of Jesus' healing of the child possessed by a speechless spirit
(Mk 9:14–29).

Other examples may illustrate the way in which this type can
focus on a single pronouncement of Jesus (Mk 2:23–28, 3:31–
35, 6:1–6, 10:13–16, 12:38–44) or on a growing, at times re-
tarded or resisted perception of an aspect of Jesus' mission (Mk
2:1–12, 5:21–43, 6:32–44/52, and 8:1–9/11–21, 12:18–27). A
miraculous intervention may motivate questions or challenges
addressed to Jesus (Mk 1:21–28, 39–45, 4:35–41, 6:45–51, 7:31–
37, 11:12–14/20–25) or a specific setting or circumstance pro-

vide the opportunity for a declaration by Jesus (Mk 2:14–17, 23–28, 10:35–45).

Dialog narratives appear in the Elijah/Elisha Narrative in similar profusion and range of narrative execution. In shorter ones a pronouncement by the prophet is motivated by a powerful deed, as in the story of Elisha's healing of the waters of Jericho (2 Kgs 2:19–21) or of his miraculous feeding of a hundred people with twenty loaves (2 Kgs 4:42–44). The longer compositions narratively frame and develop conversations between the prophet and his partners, as in the narration of Elisha's raising a sunken axe (2 Kgs 6:1–7) or of his orders to King Joash to carry out symbolic acts with bow and arrows (2 Kgs 13:14–19/22–25); on the other hand, the narration of the prophet's staged encounters with the Shunammite woman motivates a variety of exchanges (2 Kgs 4:8–37).

This broad, formal correspondence between dialog narratives in the two writings is accompanied by variations in narrative execution. Suffice it to note similar formal and thematic correlations as well as variations between corresponding dialog narratives occurring in the Elijah Story (1 Kgs 17:1–2 Kgs 1:18) and in the Elisha Narrative (2 Kgs 2:1–13:25), illustrated by a comparison of the two stories on the motif "revival of the only child of a faithful woman who hosts the prophet" (1 Kgs 17:17–24/2 Kgs 4:18–37).

4.2.3 Vision-Audition Stories

Units of the vision-audition type make the interaction between the terrestrial and the celestial spheres the narrative motivation for a divine pronouncement in relation to Jesus' mission. The three examples in Mk are placed at the beginning, middle, and end of the gospel: the stories of Jesus' baptism, his transfiguration, and his resurrection (Mk 1:9–11, 9:2–9, 16:1–8). In this manner they validate Jesus' role on earth at the three transition points between the four acts of Mk's plot. The reception of words of a heavenly voice is in each instance the central element.

Thus in the transfiguration story it is granted to Peter, James, and John, three named male disciples, and in the resurrection story the recipients are Mary Magdalene, Mary wife of James, and Salome, three named female followers. In the baptism narrative it is evidently only Jesus who hears the heavenly voice identifying him as God's beloved son.

It is as much thematic as formal correspondence that reminds Mk's audience of two similarly placed visionary stories in the Elisha Narrative (2 Kgs 2:1–13:25). At its beginning Elisha is granted the sight of Elijah's assumption at the Jordan, conveying on the former the spirit of the latter (2 Kgs 2:1–18). Then, as the narration of Elisha's deeds of power (2 Kgs 2:1–8:6) draws to its close, another story with a visionary interlude appears. The narrative about the Aramaen raiders sent with "horses and chariotry" to capture Elisha (2 Kgs 6:8–23) tells of the latter's opening the eyes of his servant who is afraid when he discovers the raiders surrounding Dothan, the city where they both are staying. The vision allows the disciple to see "the mountain full of horses and fiery chariotry, surrounding Elisha," in this manner vindicating the prophet's earlier claim that "there are more on our side than on theirs." Moreover, while the last part of the Elisha Narrative does not contain a further vision, it does employ the motif "resurrection from a tomb" (2 Kgs 13:20–21; comp. Mk 16:1–8) as well as the direct reference to a phrase that in Elisha's first and second vision stories identifies the object of the trans-terrestrial sight: "Horses and fiery chariotry" (comp. 2 Kgs 13:14 with 2:12 and 6:17).

In sum, the correspondence between Mk and 2 Kgs 2:1–13:25 in relation to the appearance of vision-audition narratives and their placements is noteworthy and an aspect of the special relationship between the two writings.

4.2.4 *Action Episodes*

Not all narrative units provide instruction through explicit pronouncements or exchanges. In both Mk and 1 Kgs 17–2 Kgs 13 are found short units that narrate only action. In the gospel Jesus' healing of Peter's mother-in-law (Mk 1:29–31) is an example; two others are the summary reports of the healing of many, either at evening or at the Sea of Galilee (Mk 1:32–34, 6:53–56; comp. 3:7–12). In the Elisha Narrative brief, purely reporting texts occur as well: examples are Elisha's parting of the Jordan at the beginning of his public career and, at its end, the revival of a corpse through accidental contact with his bones (2 Kgs 2:14, 13:20–21). Similarly the appearance of editorial comments or transition passages in both writings may be noted; but their correspondences are not sufficiently unique to warrant identification and discussion in this context.

4.3 Scene Combinations

Within the comprehensive design of Mk's four acts individual scenes may be related to each other in a manner that heightens narrative effect. In the following discussion some three ways are noted due to their correspondence to similar scene combinations in the Elijah/Elisha Narrative. The doubling of the miraculous feeding of thousands has cumulative force in that it presents the disciples' lack of comprehension after the first as lamentable, but after the second as reprehensible (see 2.6 above). On the other hand, individual units may also be juxtaposed so as to create a series on a similar theme, such as the controversy stories of Mk 2:1–3:6. Finally, scenes may be combined in such a manner that one frames another, as in the story of Jesus' intervention on behalf of Jairus' daughter, the narration of which both precedes and follows that of the healing of the hemorrhaging woman (Mk 5:21–43). Each of these ways of connecting scenes calls for discussion in light of parallels in 1 Kgs 17–2 Kgs 13.

4.3.1 Doubling

The progressive-cumulative effect of scene duplication has been noted as a tell-tale feature of one of the indicator passages (8:21;

see 2.6 above). Through it the gospel leads the disciples (and with them, the readers) to reflection on the significance of this compositional procedure. Alerted to the special import of the Elijah/Elisha Narrative, the audience recalls that Elisha not only repeated his forerunner's feat of miraculously supplying food to a faithful woman and her offspring who found themselves in straits (comp. 2 Kgs 4:1–7 with 1 Kgs 17:8–16), but also that then Elisha duplicated his own deed of power by feeding a hundred persons miraculously (2 Kgs 4:42–44). The same pattern is repeated in relation to Elisha's bringing to life the dead: Like the man from Tishbe the son of Shaphat revived the deceased child of a woman who had hosted him (comp. 2 Kgs 4:18–37 with 1 Kgs 17:17–24), only to double the miracle in the revival of a corpse who had accidentally touched the prophet's bones (2 Kgs 13:20–21).

Thus doubling is suggestive: As scriptural duplication of motif related scenes signifies continuance and heightening in narrative execution, so the gospel's doubling projects continuance and still further heightening of the inherited pattern. It is noteworthy that in Mk's third part (Mk 8:1–15:39) a scene of giving sight, appearing once in the Elisha Narrative (2 Kgs 6:17[8–23]), appears doubled in the two stories of Jesus' giving sight to blind men: Mk 8:22–26/10:46–52. A progressive element is also evident there: While the first restoration of sight is two-staged and tells of Jesus' several actions and words, the other is instantaneous and highlights the blind man's eager initiative; while the first man healed was sent away, the second followed his benefactor.

4.3.2 Serialization

Mk offers several examples of the combination of individual scenes through serialization. Thus Mk 2:1–3:6 contains five controversy stories (2:1–12, 13–17, 18–22, 23–28; 3:1–6), each unfolding, it seems, the motif of opposition between prophet and the people's leaders (2 Kgs 3:13–14; see the motif discussion in 6.2.1 below). They are combined in order to provide a preview of aspects of Jesus' new teaching, in the same manner as a similar controversy series will do at the end of Jesus' public activity (Mk 11:27–12:44: 11:27–33 (15–18); 12:1–12, 13–17, 18–27, 28–34, 35–37, 38–44).

Further serializations include the following: Jesus' successive and parallel calls of the first two disciple pairs (Mk 1:16–18, 19–20), each of which is based on Elijah's call of Elisha (1 Kgs 19:19–21); Jesus' three parallel discourses on the offending hand, foot, and eye (Mk 9:43, 45, 47), each of which is based on the motif of the offending hand of the Syrian officer cured by Elisha from leprosy (2 Kgs 5:18; comp. 6.2.3 below); the two negatively qualified comparisons of the Kingdom of God with a patch of new cloth on an old coat and with new wine in old skins (Mk 2:22, 23); the coordination of five parables in Mk 4:1–34 (comp. 2.4 above); and the condemnation of Jesus in Jerusalem on the basis of a sequence of two trials, that before the religious authority and that before the secular power (Mk 14:1–15:1; 15:2–37) — a serialization based, it seems, on the false claim against Naboth alleging that he had cursed "God and King," understood as warranting two trials (comp. 1 Kgs 21:10, 13; see 6.2.3 below).

The escalating effect of serialization of story units is evident, though not prominent, in 1 Kgs 17–2 Kgs 13. Examples are the two (three) short dialog narratives that portray Elisha miraculously dealing with food for the benefit of faithful persons (2 Kgs [4:1–7], 4:38–41, 42–44) and the sequence of three Elijah stories that demonstrate the superiority of Israel's God over the Canaanite god Baal: (*a*) as giver of rain and fertility (1 Kgs 17:1–18:46), (*b*) as guarantor of justice (1 Kgs 21:1–29), and (*c*) as the one who grants healing and health (2 Kgs 1:2–17). Moreover, the story of the king's request addressed to Gehazi, "to rehearse all the great deeds which Elisha has done" (2 Kgs 8:1–6), narratively confirms the cumulative-persuasive force of the servant's recital through the providential arrival of the Shunamite woman, whose appearance validates his words.

4.3.3 Framing

Through the device of framing, one unit comes to be encased within another. Thus the story in Mk 5:21–43 opens with Jairus' urgent invitation to Jesus to come to his house and to heal his sick daughter. But while on the road Jesus is delayed by his healing of the hemorrhaging woman. Thus when he finally arrives at Jairus' house, the child has died. His intervention revives her, and thus presumably heightens the miracle in relation to merely healing her, as originally requested by her father. This employment of the compositional device seems based on a longer narrative unit in the Elisha Narrative: that of his journey to the Shunamite woman's house in response to her request to bring her dead son back to life (2 Kgs 4:18–37). The encasement pattern of Mk 5:21–43 is seminally present in that narrative unit: Like Jairus to Jesus, so the woman comes to the prophet after the journey from her home to request his intervention. When she reaches the prophet's residence she finds herself about to be rebuffed by Gehazi, Elisha's servant. In desperation she clings to the prophet's feet and so touches the man of God; after he has intervened with Gehazi on her behalf, he proceeds to act on her request.

There are further examples in Mk. The story of Jesus' cleansing of the Temple (Mk 11:15–18, 27–33) and that of his cursing of the fig tree (Mk 11:12–14, 20–24) frame each other and thus create an interaction. Jesus' Temple cleansing is authenticated by the withering of the fig tree, which, it seems, represents the dying order; in turn, the same act is evidence of the inception of a new order. Another instance is the encasement of the narrative of the God-pleasing but impactless martyrdom of John the Baptist (Mk 6:14–29) within that of Jesus' sending out and receiving the twelve disciples (Mk 6:7–13/30–31). The frame supplied to that innocent death by this successful mission signals that Jesus accomplished what John did not, and the man from Nazareth stands once more authenticated as the bringer of the Kingdom of God.

Explicit compositional framing appears several times in the
Elijah/Elisha Narrative. Thus the opening (and later repeated)
statement of the man of God concerning the duration of the
divinely sent drought and the report of its end frame a cluster of Elijah stories (1 Kgs 17:1/17:2–18:40 [18:1]/41–46). Similarly the narration of King Ahab's sin and his prophetically
announced violent death provide the frame for the Micaiah, son
of Imlah, story, which gives to Ahab's fate a sinister, puzzling
aspect: it is divinely permitted deception that brought him low
(1 Kgs 21:1–29/22:2–28/29–40)! Finally, in light of the evangelist's use of the framing device in relation to Jesus' Temple cleansing it is noteworthy that King Joash' entrance into
and eventual restoration of the Temple frames the story of the
overthrow of apostasy in Jerusalem(2 Kgs 11:1–12 [18] /11:13–
12:4/12:5–17).

Chapter 5

Narrative Motifs

Alerted to the transparency of the gospel's story line to that of a scriptural model, readers are prompted to consider in a new manner also details in narrative execution. Questions such as these arise: Why do some unusual and seemingly unmotivated words and notions appear, such as Judas' kiss of betrayal or Jesus' order to "go, sell" everything? What considerations lead the evangelist to introduce a reference to an obscure deity such as Beelzebul? Do certain quantitatively defined concepts, such as Jesus' prohibiting the disciples to take "money and two cloaks," suggest that narrative constraints are at work? Furthermore, are plots of some of the individual story units, such as that of Jesus' healing a stretcherbound paralytic who had been let down from the roof of a house, or of Jesus' discourse on purity of hand and heart, shaped by similar plot elements in the scriptural paradigm? Finally, are also sequences of scenes, such as the five controversy stories at the beginning of the gospel or, at its end, the narration of Jesus' fateful confrontation with his adversaries, composed in the light of biblical precedent?

These and other examples of narrative correspondence will now be discussed, beginning with those limited in scope to a word, a phrase, or a numerical value (chapter 5), and proceeding to correlations in scene plots and sequences (chapter 6). Their parallelizations and contextualizations in Mk illuminate not only narrative motivations but also, cumulatively, aspects of what may be called the gospel's scriptural depth.

5.1   Words and Phrases

Some words and phrases in Mk stand out because they seem unusual or unmotivated. Why did Judas betray his master with a kiss? Why is Jesus alleged to be mad? Why can a proselyte be compared to a dog? By the same token, why do some noteworthy phrases occur, at times repeatedly, such as Jesus' order to "go, sell" everything, or the disclaimer of any association with another person, "What have you and I to do with each other?" or cries of the dying Jesus "with a loud voice"? What makes these words and phrases objects of inquiry is the observation that they also appear in the Elijah/Elisha Narrative, where they similarly stand out as details of narrative execution. The following analysis seeks to support the case for their employment in the gospel as carriers of its correspondence to a scriptural model.

5.1.1   The Kiss of Betrayal

Why does Judas choose to identify his master to the captors through the sign of a kiss? Set into the sustained narration of Jesus' martyrdom (Mk 14:1–15:39) are these two scenes: Jesus' announcement of his betrayal by one of the twelve disciples (Mk 14:17–21) and, after the last joint meal and the events in Gethsemane, the narration of Judas' act of betrayal and Jesus' capture (Mk 14:43–46). The announcement scene reveals only the fact of the future act of disloyalty but discloses neither the identity of the betrayer (but note Mk 3:19) nor the manner in which he will carry out his design. The last of the Gethsemane scenes then proceeds not only to name the betrayer but also to describe how he will carry out his plan: He will identify the one whom the captors seek through a kiss. The sign of the kiss as the means of identification is not motivated; one would expect

an identifying word or a pointing gesture as the means of sin-
gling Jesus out from his disciples. Moreover, the use of this sign
is marked by irony because a gesture commonly expressing loyalty and devotion here serves to denote abandonment and gross
disloyalty! Hence the question: Does the kiss of betrayal convey
to the audience more than meets the eye? Is its employment
due to the presence of the motif in 1 Kgs 17–2 Kgs 13? The
answer is, it seems, affirmative.

After receiving at Mount Horeb divine instructions concerning the overthrow of apostasy he is to set in motion (1 Kgs
19:15–17), Elijah is assured that 7,000 will be left as a remnant
in Israel, "all knees who have not bowed before Baal and every
mouth who has not kissed him" (1 Kgs 19:18). What connects
this text with Mk 14:43–45 is the concept of the kiss as sign of
betrayal, of Jesus in the latter passage, of the God of Israel in
the former. The corresponding motif contextualizations suggest
that the evangelist presents Judas' betrayal as sign of apostasy,
like its scriptural counterpart deprived of a future, and in this
manner makes the gospel transparent to its model in the Hebrew Scriptures. By the same token, the readers' awareness of
this correlation motivates Judas' kiss of betrayal.

5.1.2 The Madness of Jesus

After the narration of Jesus' appointment of twelve disciples
(Mk 3:13–19) and of the pressure of the crowd on him after the
return to his residence "so that they could not even eat" (Mk
3:20), two reactions to the man from Nazareth are told: According to the first (Mk 3:21), "those siding with him went out
to seize him because they were assuming [literally: saying] that
he was mad." Neither Jesus' response to this initiative nor an
actual seizure is narrated—quite in contrast to the second reaction, according to which theologians who hail from Jerusalem
claim that "he has Beelzebul" or "an unclean spirit" (Mk 3:22–
30). The motif of Jesus' madness must leave readers puzzled
because the gospel introduces but does not pursue it. To be

sure, its general narrative motivation may be seen in the preceding reference to the public, large, and positive response of the people to Jesus' activity (Mk 3:20, comp. 1:32–34, 3:7–12) but also in the emerging — and ominous — hostility of leading circles to him (Mk 3:6, 22, 30).

The Elijah/Elisha Narrative is able to throw light on the appearance of the motif in Mk. In its third part (2 Kgs 8:7–12:17) the notion of the "mad" behavior of figures instrumental in the overthrow of apostasy occurs twice: When Jehu, who just had secretly been anointed king over Israel by a prophetic emissary of Elisha, is queried by his fellow officers about the secretive visitor, they refer to him as "that mad man." Jehu's first response seeks to cover up what happened with the comment, "You know the man and his talk" (2 Kgs 9:11 [1–13]). A little later, when Jehu's hasty drive with his co-conspirators to the royal summer residence is narrated, the lookout man in Jezreel's gate is eventually able to identify the approaching troupe as headed by Jesu son of Nimshi, because he drives "madly" (2 Kgs 9:20 [14–20]). Thus the motif of the madness of the LORD's protagonists is prominent in the part of 1 Kgs 17–2 Kgs 13 that relates the final confrontation of Israel's God with apostasy.

Is its appearance in Mk another connection of the latter to the former? If so, its positive qualification in relation to those commissioned to bring the divine rule explains its attribution to Jesus by those who side with him (if this is the meaning of the prepositional phrase used here) as well as the lack of a narrative follow-up. By the same token, its occurrence near the gospel's beginning, and within texts that describe serious opposition to Jesus and thus prepare the audience for the eventual confrontation, points to the latter as the necessary sequel of Jesus' public activity (comp. Mk 3:6). In this case the attempted seizure must be understood as an attempt to protect Jesus from that confrontation either altogether (comp. Peter's reaction to Jesus' announcement of his future martyrdom, Mk 8:32b–33) or before the point in time that the scriptural paradigm assigns to it (note the references to a time in the future and to Jerusalem in connection with Jesus' death in Mk 8:31, 9:31, and 10:32–34). It seems that the double occurrence of the madness motif in 2 Kgs 8:7–12:17 is the foil of the motif of Jesus' madness.

5.1.3 The Comparison of Proselytes to Dogs

Jesus' exorcism of the unclean spirit from the daughter of the Syrophoenician woman (Mk 7:24–30) is preceded by a remarkable exchange. To the mother's request for intervention Jesus responds that first "the children" are to be fed, "for it is not fitting to take the bread from the children and to throw it to the little dogs." The woman counters in the same vein, "Lord, also the little dogs eat under the table from the crumbs of the children." This response prompts Jesus to acquiesce: "On account of this word go (to your home) — the spirit has left your daughter."

The story evidently illustrates an exception made by Jesus to the notion that Israel ("the children") has first claim on the benefits of Jesus' mission; only after it has received what is its due may non-Israelites ("the little dogs") share in what Jesus offers. The Gentile woman employs that imagery in a striking turnabout: The temporally conceived succession is transformed into a spatial juxtaposition that softens but does not eliminate it. But why do both Jesus and the woman use without explanation the offensive term with reference to non-Israelites? Does the self-characterization of the Syrian Hazael as "dog" in one of the Elisha stories provide the clue? When the prophet on his way to Damascus encounters Hazael, who had been sent by his sick king Ben-hadad to enquire of him concerning the illness, Elisha proceeds to announce to Hazael his future exploits (2 Kgs 8:7–15; comp. 1 Kgs 19:15–17). When Hazael responds in surprise with the words, "What is your servant, the dog, that he should accomplish this great thing?" he is told by Elisha that in a vision the LORD has shown him as king over Aram — a prediction the fulfilment of which the narrative hastens to tell.

The Syrian's self-predication as "the dog," in apposition to the phrase "your servant," underscores his subordinate role in relation to the prophet who makes and unmakes kings. By the same token, readers who are aware of the evangelist's use of the term in Mk 7:24–30 cannot help but note that the word refers to Hazael as a non-Israelite who lets himself be directed by the God of Israel in a matter of life and death, who is assured of divine intervention even before Israel, "the children," in its entirety is vouchsafed the overthrow of apostasy and the full establishment of the LORD's rule, and who is portrayed as a notable proselyte. That scriptural backdrop provides for Mk's use of the term the narrative motivation as well as the plot of the story.

5.1.4 The Order to "Go, Sell"

The respectful inquiry by a well-to-do man as to what he is to do in order to inherit eternal life is eventually countered by Jesus with reference to six of "the commandments." When the man assures him that he has observed these from his youth, Jesus is drawn to him and observes that he still needs to do one more thing: "Go, sell what you have and give [the proceeds] to the poor, and you will have a treasure in the heavens. Then come, follow me!" But the inquirer does not wish to do this and leaves saddened (Mk 10:17–22; comp. 23–31).

The two imperatives with which Jesus begins his last response, while narratively motivated, stand out due both to their asyndetic juxtaposition (followed by two further, syndetically linked imperative forms) and to the radical demand it makes of the well-to-do inquirer. But it is the unexpected phrase, "go, sell!" that reminds readers already alerted to the gospel's special relationship to the Elijah/Elisha Narrative of a like formulation there: After a prophet's widow had implored Elisha for help to ward off her husband's creditors and had carried out Elisha's order to fill her own as well as borrowed vessels with oil poured from her cruse, he commands her, "Go, sell the oil and give [the proceeds] to your creditors, then you and your son will live from what is left" (2 Kgs 4:1–7). To be sure, the plots of the two stories seem at first quite different, but a second look shows that in both the acquisition of life, qualified in a certain manner, is the issue. For the widow and her sons it is survival into the age of the divine rule that Elisha will soon initiate; for the inquirer it is "eternal life" (literally, the life of the age to come). In sum, phrase and theme correspondence supply yet another conceptual and phraseological link between the gospel and 1 Kgs 17–2 Kgs 13.

5.1.5   The Disclaimer of Association

Twice the evangelist employs the same rhetorical question in order to identify the dissociation of unclean spirits from Jesus. His first teaching session in the Synagogue of Capernaum is followed by a deed of power: the exorcism of an unclean spirit from a man present in the house of worship (Mk 1:21–28). The story relates that it is the mere presence of Jesus that prompts the unclean spirit to address him with the words, "What have we and you to do with each other, Jesus the Nazarene? Have you come to destroy us? I know who you are: The Holy One of God." However, upon Jesus' command to leave the man, the spirit contorts him and departs with a loud cry, so that those present begin to wonder about this "new teaching in power." The same formulation appears in the narrative of the Gerasene demoniac (Mk 5:1–20). The unclean spirit, on becoming aware of Jesus' proximity, makes the man come close, genuflect, and, having uttered a loud cry, says, "What have you and I to do with each other, Jesus, son of God the Highest? I implore you by God not to torment me." Also in this story Jesus exorcises the spirit.

The rhetorical question with which both unclean spirits begin their words directed to Jesus is the very phrase with which the widow of Zarephath opens her challenging words to Elijah, her guest, after her son had become ill to the point of death (1 Kgs 17:8–24): "What have I and you to do with each other, man of God? You have come to cause my sins to be remembered and to bring death to my son!" The Tishbite, however, after prayer to the LORD and certain actions designed to revive the child, brings him to life again. At that point the widow responds that now she has come to recognize that he is indeed a man of God and that the LORD's word is in truth spoken by him.

What connects the two Markan stories to that Elijah narrative is not only the same rhetorical question with which a distraught person opens an address to a challenger, but also the same person's eventual recognition of the true identity of the challenger. Thus the widow in the end identifies the Tishbite as a legitimate representative of Israel's God, and the two unclean spirits recognize in Jesus either "the Holy One of God" or "the son of God the Highest." Moreover, in both gospel stories the spirit either leaves the possessed person (Mk 1:26) or speaks up (Mk 5:6) "with a loud voice" — a phrase that reoccurs, again doubled, in the passion story (Mk 15:34, 37). That further connection between scriptural paradigm and Mk now claims our attention.

5.1.6 Jesus' Last Cries "With a Loud Voice"

The phrase "with a loud voice" appears not only twice toward the beginning of the gospel (Mk 1:24, 5:7), but also twice at its end: Six hours after Jesus' crucifixion, when darkness had fallen over the whole land for three hours, Jesus called out in Hebrew with a loud voice the first line of Ps 22 (Mk 15:34); bystanders who misunderstood that cry wondered whether he had called Elijah. Then the narrative tells of Jesus' demise after he had again called out "with a loud voice" (Mk 15:37). The phrase as well as its doubled presence is paralleled in the story of Elijah's encounter with the Baal prophets on Mount Carmel (1 Kgs 18:1–46). At midday the Tishbite mocks his adversaries, who remain without a sign of their god's intervention; he does so with the words, "Call [him] with a loud voice because he is a god...." The narration then tells of their efforts, using the

same phrase, "Then they called with a loud voice..." (1 Kgs
18:27, 28) — ultimately of no avail. It is noteworthy that the
doubled occurrences of the phrase in Mk's passion story and in
the story of Elijah's encounter with apostasy both appear in
the context of an ordeal in which the intervention of the God
of Israel on behalf of his servants is the issue, though the two
narratives diverge in the description of that divine action (comp.
1 Kgs 18:38–39 with Mk 15:38–39, 42–46, 16:1–8).

5.2   Numbers, Names, and Roles

The words and phrases discussed in the preceding section appear
in a different, new light when viewed against the backdrop of the
Elijah/Elisha Narrative. Their employment in the gospel provides a specific scriptural quality to its composition, reinforcing
the readers' perception of its continuity with, and transformation of, its literary-conceptual antecedent. This is also evident
in several quantitatively defined notions, such as Peter's "triple"
denial of his master before the cock crows "twice" or the "hundredfold" yield of seeds sown (see 2.7 and 2.4 above). Other
numerically defined notions that invite examination in the light
of 1 Kgs 17–2 Kgs 13 are Jesus' "forty-day withdrawal into the
wilderness," his initial call of "four disciples," and the prohibition, found in the directions given to the twelve disciples for
their mission, "not to take along money and two cloaks." By
the same token, certain unusual proper names and references to
social roles appear both in the Elijah/Elisha Narrative and in
the gospel, notably "Beelzebul" and "Tyre and Sidon," as well
as "widow" and "leper."

5.2.1   Jesus' Forty Days in the Wilderness

Mk concludes its initial part with a brief narration of Jesus'
undergoing a test before he begins his public activity: He is
conveyed by the spirit into the wilderness where he is tempted

by Satan for the duration of the forty days he is "with the animals" and finds himself served by "angels" (Mk 1:12–13). The unit is in part patterned through motifs drawn from the first section of the Elijah Narrative (1 Kgs 17–19). Specifically, Jesus' forty-day stay in the desert corresponds in its numerical aspect to Elijah's flight from Queen Jezebel's threat of death, engaging him in a wilderness journey of forty days and nights to Mount Horeb; like the Tishbite Jesus goes alone and is supported by celestial emissaries (1 Kgs 19:1–7). The evangelist does not say of what Satan's temptation consisted; do the divine challenge of the man of God at the sacred mountain and his reception of the order to set in motion that train of events that eventually led to the re-establishment of the LORD's rule in Israel and Judah (1 Kgs 19:4–18) provide the horizon of understanding to be evoked? At any rate, Jesus is portrayed as tested and validated as Elijah of old. If this is the case, the narrative connection of Jesus with Elijah rather than exclusively with Elisha (comp. 2.1 above) seems to be an inconsistency. What evidently matters is the cumulation of motifs from 1 Kgs 17–2 Kgs 13 on Jesus in such a manner that he appears to transcend both Elijah and Elisha; plot correspondence takes precedence over correlation in figures of the cast.

5.2.2 Four Discoverers of the Gospel

The brief narration of the call of the first two disciple pairs (Mk 1:16–20) is built on the motif of "the disclosure of the good news and its four bearers" as found in its model text of 2 Kgs 7:3–16. Thus the first announcement of the gospel, triggered by the forerunner's arrest (Mk 1:14–15), is followed by the constitution of the group of persons who are its first carriers. They are "four" in number, thus alluding to the four lepers who, according to the scriptural antecedent, stood ready to become the bearers of the "good news" of Samaria's unexpected, miraculous reprieve from the Aramean siege. Simon and Andrew, James and John appear together in the gospel — and, by the same token, separated from

the other disciples — only once again: they are the exclusive
recipients of their master's instruction about the time and the
signs of the coming Temple destruction (Mk 13:3). For the
evangelist the number of the initial disciples is, as it were, a
canonical one, and that in marked contrast to the identification
of five first disciples in Jn 1:35–51.

5.2.3   The Prohibition of Money and Two Cloaks

Jesus' directions to "the Twelve" set forth what they must and
must not take on their missionary journey (Mk 6:8–9). Framed
by references to a staff and to sandals appears the prohibition
"not to take along money nor two cloaks." This peculiar combination of specified objects is paralleled by a narrative motif
in the story told in 2 Kgs 5. After Elisha had cured the Syrian
commander Naaman of leprosy, he refused to accept in payment any of the valuables the cleansed man had brought and
dismissed him with a blessing. On the other hand, Elisha's servant Gehazi had witnessed his master's actions and sought to
gain for himself what his master had refused. He ran after the
Syrian and, under the pretext that two prophets newly arrived
from another prophetic settlement were indigent, asked for "a
talent of silver and two cloaks" (2 Kgs 5:22). While he succeeds
in deceiving Naaman and sets out to hide the objects in his own
tent, his master Elisha knows of the act of greed, confronts him,
and afflicts him with leprosy. Evidently here a prophet's disciple
seeks to enrich himself with money and two cloaks. Thus the
gospel evokes through this formulation the memory of scriptural
antecedent and so employs the motif as a sinister reinforcement
of Jesus' directives.

5.2.4   The Reference to Beelzebul

In Mk 3:22–30 the accusation of theologians from Jerusalem
that Jesus "has Beelzebul," and thus accomplishes his deeds of
power through Satan, calls forth Jesus' response in the form of

instruction. He speaks in parables to those whom he had called to listen to him, then discourses about a kingdom that cannot endure if it is internally divided, and concludes by condemning the sin of blasphemy against the Holy Spirit. The evangelist ends the unit by noting that the response was given to counter the claim that Jesus had "an unclean spirit" — the claim evidently synonymous with the earlier claim that the man from Nazareth was the agent of a foreign god whose name the Hebrew Scriptures contain.

Baal-zebub is, according to the story of Elijah's encounter with the emissaries of King Ahaziah of Israel (2 Kgs 1:2–17a), the name of the god of Ekron, one of the Philistine cities in the coastal plain (2 Kgs 1:2, 3, 6, 16). Thus it is a foreign deity, and the embassy of an Israelite king sent to inquire of him concerning his paralysis after a fall from the roof of his palace is an act of apostasy; this is the burden of Elijah's words of chastisement addressed to the king's messengers. In keeping with that Elijah story Jesus' challengers identify the god of Ekron with Satan, the chief of the antidivine forces (Mk 3:23–25). As far as Mk's narrative execution is concerned, the references to the latter and, at the end of the unit, to the claim that Jesus is possessed by "an unclean spirit" (Mk 3:30) would suffice as narrative motivation for Jesus' response. Thus it seems that the personification of the antidivine forces as Beelzebul serves to provide a specific connection to the gospel's model story.

5.2.5 Jesus' Sojourn near Tyre and Sidon

The narrative of Jesus' exorcism of the unclean spirit possessing the Syrophoenician woman's daughter (Mk 7:24–30) locates the miracle near "Tyre and Sidon" (the second city name does not appear in the uncial manuscript D [5th cent. C.E.] but is found in the three uncials Sinaiticus [4th cent.], Alexandrinus [5th cent.], and Vaticanus [4th cent.]). The reference to this area north of Galilee, and specifically to Sidon, alerts the readers to a story at the beginning of the Elijah/Elisha Narrative. It is that of

Elijah's sojourn with the widow in Zarephath "which belongs to Sidon" (1 Kgs 17:8–16). When the Man of God arrived in that town, he encountered a widow who readily responded to his request for some water. When he also asked for bread, she told him that she had only left enough flour and oil to prepare a last meal for herself and her son; after that, she continued, they will have to die. Elijah, however, asked her to do as she planned except that she first make a small loaf for him. In that case the LORD's word assures her that her jar and jug will not become empty as long as the famine lasts. The narrator concludes with the observation that this indeed happened after the woman had acceded to Elijah's request.

The narrative in Mk is compositionally related to that story in that both signal through the use of the city name "Sidon" that they are set in the area of the Phoenician cities to the north of the land of Israel, in that both have the holy man intervene on behalf of a woman and her child, and in that both contain a dialogue in which initial resistance is overcome — by the woman in the Elijah story but by Jesus in the gospel narrative (see the discussion in 5.1.3 above of the comparison of proselytes to "the little dogs" in Mk 7:27, 28).

5.2.6 The Cleansing of a Leper

The text unit Mk 1:40–45 narrates as Jesus' third miracle the cleansing of a leper. It is told in some detail and contains a dialogue as well as an order given by Jesus. The sick man challenges the master with the statement that if he wishes, he can free him from the disease. Jesus, in turn, is moved by compassion, touches the man, and responds that he indeed wishes him to be made well. Immediately the leprosy leaves him. Jesus then orders him to present himself to the priest with the customary offering, but otherwise to remain silent. That, however, does not happen and the man from Nazareth becomes even more known and beset by people.

The story has received its theme "cleansing of leprosy" from the narrative of Elisha's healing of the leprosy of the Syrian commander Naaman (2 Kgs 5:1–19). This motif appears once each in the Elijah/Elisha Narrative and in Mk; the gospel employs it near its beginning in order to indicate to those "who have ears to hear" (Mk 4:23) the correspondence between the story and its model in the scriptural paradigm. Moreover, the leper challenges Jesus with the words, "If you wish, you can cleanse me!" Through the expression of this sentiment the evangelist reminds the readers of a similar one that informed Naaman's approach to Elisha (comp. Mk 1:41 with 2 Kgs 5:9–12).

5.2.7 The Commendation of a Widow

The text unit Mk 12:38–44 points to the Temple as the spatial setting of Jesus' discourse. His warning against the theologians who practice their profession with pomp and pretense serves as the foil against which the selfless donation of the widow for the Temple's upkeep is praised. Moreover, the triple reference to the offering box at the Temple entrance serves as signal that the evangelist returns to the compositional sequencing that 2 Kgs 12:5–17 lays out: Temple restoration — Temple upkeep (comp. 2 Kgs 12:5–9/10–17).

Jesus castigates six different actions of the clergy. The first four relate to various exploitations of the respect that people accord them; the fifth is their "eating up widows' houses," and the sixth is prayer made in public. Then Jesus seats himself opposite the collection box of the worshippers' freewill offering. He observes that many well-to-do persons put into it large sums, but also that a poor widow offers two copper coins. This prompts him solemnly to tell his disciples that this woman has given more than all the others: While they gave out of their wealth, she offered what little she called her own, "all her means of livelihood." The theme of the unit is the contrast between members of the clergy who exploit their office for personal gain and the widow who donates all that she has. Both motifs are drawn from 1 Kgs 17–2 Kgs 13. In one of its narratives King Joash's

ordering of the affairs of the Temple in order to counteract the
clergy's selfishness is told (2 Kgs 12:5–10). Another story near
the beginning of the Elijah/Elisha Narrative concerns a poor
widow who, though she finds herself in a near hopeless situation, acts with great generosity toward the Man of God (1 Kgs
17:8–16[24]). The warnings of the discourse in Mk 12:38–44
echo the widow motif. This is also expressed stylistically: the
word "widow" appears thrice in both Mk 12:38–44 as well as in
its model (1 Kgs 17:9, 10, 20). Furthermore, the second appearance of the "poor widow" motif in the Elijah/Elisha Narrative
(2 Kgs 4:1–7) tells of a creditor who soon after a widow's husband's death comes to claim her two sons, now the mainstay of
her life, as his slaves. The prophet's intervention prevents the
creditor from putting an end to her family's existence.

Chapter 6

Narrative Plots

6.1 Individual Stories

Not only specific words and phrases, names and numbers make a case for a unique relation between the gospel and its scriptural model, but also the story lines of individual units in Mk correspond to some found in 1 Kgs 17–2 Kgs 13. The following examination of six texts illustrates the nature of their use by the evangelist: Jesus' healing of the stretcherbound paralytic who is let down through the roof of the house where the man from Nazareth was surrounded by a crowd (Mk 2:1–12), Jesus' discourses on the purity of hand and heart when challenged in relation to some of his disciples' failure to purify themselves before meals (Mk 7:1–23), and his teaching on gaining and loosing one's life as his follower (Mk 8:34–35), and on the sign of the end of the present age (Mk 13:1–37). Finally, the narrations of Jesus' setting in order the affairs of the Temple (Mk 11:15–17) as well as of the inability of his women followers to locate his body in the cave in which Joseph of Arimathea had sought to preserve it (Mk 15:40–16:8) will be discussed.

6.1.1 The Faith of the Paralytic

The story of Jesus' healing of the paralyzed man brought to him on a stretcher (Mk 2:1–12) is his fourth deed of power. In recognition of the faith of the man and of those who carried his stretcher — a faith so persistent that they even broke open the roof of the house in order to gain access to the man they sought — Jesus assures the sick man: "Child, your sins are forgiven." However, through this act Jesus also challenges some of the theologians who witnessed the encounter and inwardly accused him of blasphemy, because they hold that the forgiveness of sins is reserved for God. Jesus knows their thoughts and addresses them with the declaration that the Son of Man has power to forgive sins also on earth, then proves his claim by ordering the paralytic to lift up his stretcher and walk. When he does so, all are amazed, praise God, and affirm that they have never before seen anything like it.

Several aspects of the story suggest that the narrative of King Ahaziah's fatal fall from his palace roof (2 Kgs 1:2–17a) serves as model. There is first the reference to the monarch's accident, which confines him to his bed, then his enquiry directed to Baal-zebub of Ekron, a foreign god (comp. the discussion of the Beelzebul reference [Mk 3:22] in 5.2.4 above), followed by the prophet's condemnation of the king's apostasy, and finally Ahaziah's death due to his lack of faith in the God of Israel.

The evangelist employs this plot as basis, varying and inverting it. While the king fell from the roof to ground level, became bedridden, and due to his own and his associates' lack of faith in the LORD has no prospect of recovery, the paralytic of Mk is lowered through the roof down to where Jesus is and, due to his own and his stretcher-carriers' faith in Jesus' healing power, finds his hope for recovery fulfilled. Thus the gospel writer uses the story line of that Elijah story as basis as well as contrast for the portrayal of Jesus' miracle and for the ensuing debate with the theologians.

6.1.2 Purity of Hand and Heart

According to Mk 7:1–23 Jesus is questioned by Pharisees and some theologians from Jerusalem concerning some of his disciples' non-observance of purification rites relating to the consumption of food. His answer begins with a quote of Is 29:13, which serves to introduce one of the theme-words for the unit: "heart" in its relation to God (Mk 7:6, 19, 21). Then Jesus accuses his challengers of the behavior that the Isaianic text chastises, specifically their substitution of the recent traditions of the elders for the will of God as codified in the Ten Commandments (Mk 7:8). By way of example he discusses the commandment enjoining filial piety, observing that the practice of (grown) children to vow as gift to the Temple objects of support they owe their parents amounts to failure to honor the latter (Mk 7:9–13). Then the disciples ask Jesus for an interpretation of "the parable" (Mk 7:17) contained in his affirmation that only what leaves the human body can defile it, not what enters it (Mk 7:14–15). Thus food, once consumed, does not affect the heart but is eliminated through digestion. But evil thoughts — some twelve kinds are listed — render a human being impure since it is they that proceed from the heart and thus are the reliable indicators of a person's impurity (Mk 7:18–23).

Evidently, the term "heart" is central in relation to that of "hand," the latter understood as indicator of the true state of the former, and not vice versa, as Jesus' challengers think. The relation between "heart" and "hand" is the theme of a short story found in 1 Kgs 17–2 Kgs 13: it is that of Jehu's encounter with the Rekabite Jehonadab when the former is on his way to Samaria in order to eliminate the remaining adherents of Baal (2 Kgs 10:15–17). Upon meeting, Jehu inquires whether "your heart [is] right with my heart as my heart is with yours?" His partner's affirmative response prompts the new king to say, "If it is, give me your hand!" This the Rekabite does, and Jehu draws him up into his chariot. Then they ride together to the capital where in zeal for the God of Israel they drown apostasy in the blood of its practitioners (2 Kgs 10:18–27).

The crucial terms are "heart," to be "in the right," and "hand." The heart as the seat of a person's mind, will, and emotion is as such not directly observable by others; its in-

tentions are ascertained through question and answer. Hence
Jehu asks Jehonadab and receives the reply that satisfies him.
Accordingly, Jehonadab's ensuing action proves that what his
handshake had signified is indeed what is in his heart. Jesus, according to Mk, argues similarly: That which the heart prompts
a person to do is the true test of its rightness, of its "purity" —
was not Jehonadab's hand its indicator?

6.1.3 Rewards of Self-Abandon

Jesus' instruction of the people and of the disciples in Mk 8:34–
9:1 deals with the price and the reward of following him. Self-
denial and loyalty to the master are the price, the acquisition
of life, and, for some, the witness of the Kingdom's coming in
power, the reward. The first discourse (Mk 8:34–38) relates
primarily to the price; the second (Mk 9:1) to the reward. Both
themes are based on motifs found in 1 Kgs 17–2 Kgs 13. Four
specific relationships between the model and its use in Mk are
explored.
  a. The statement that self-denial is the price of discipleship echoes Elisha's ready response to Elijah's call to follow him
(1 Kgs 19:19–21, comp. 15–17). The man from Abel-meholah
left the sedentary life of the farmer and the companionship of
family in order to become an itinerant Man of God like his master. Elisha even insisted on accompanying the Tishbite on his
last journey, that to his assumption, refusing three times to let
him go by himself (2 Kgs 2:1–6). Mk 8:34 enjoins that same
self-denial on Jesus' followers and suggests Elisha's discipleship
as the model (comp. also Mk 2:14, 1:16–20).
  b. In support of his statement Jesus contrasts the person
who wishes to preserve his life with the one who is prepared to
give it up. The former will loose it while the latter will gain
it (Mk 8:35). The master adds that the loss of one's life is not
outweighed by the gain of all that is in the world; one's life
cannot be ransomed (Mk 8:36–37). In short, gaining and losing
one's life may indeed be understood as appropriate aspects of

discipleship of a crucified master, though their narrative motivation is not apparent. The latter is supplied by the story of the four lepers who find themselves starving to death in the gate of besieged Samaria (2 Kgs 7:3–16). They ask each other why they should remain there without sustenance until death claims them. They argue that if they go back into the city, the famine will bring them certain death there — the same fate that will befall them if they do not go. They conclude, "Let us go over to the Arameans. If they leave us alive, we will stay alive, but if they kill us, we will die" (2 Kgs 7:4). The extremity of their situation made them ready for both life and death — and so they expressly state.

Because they risked their life, they in fact won it, discovering the good news of the Arameans' flight and of the end of the city's siege in the bargain. The readiness of the lepers for both death and life and their unexpected gain of survival is the motif to which the three related statements about "life and death" in Mk 8:35–37 point. Mk 8:35 is a direct, summarizing commentary on the biblical story while the supporting questions of Mk 8:36–37 allude to related aspects of the lepers' story. They would not have benefited from the abundance of goods that fell to them in the abandoned enemy camp had they not been ready to risk their life. Nor could they have ransomed their life from death had they not been prepared to give it up. These connections between scriptural motif and its conceptual-literary use illustrate the free manner in which the evangelist bases narration on scriptural antecedent.

c. Mark's Jesus warns that whoever is ashamed of him and of his words will find himself repudiated by the Son of Man when he appears (Mk 8:38). This statement is based on the inversion of a corresponding motif in one of the Elisha stories. According to 2 Kgs 2:1–15, the prophet insists on accompanying his master when he journeys to the Jordan in preparation for his assumption, even though Elijah thrice asks him to remain behind. Elisha's loyalty is rewarded by his being honored to see his master assumed into heaven and commissioned as his successor, endowed with a double portion of the Tishbite's spirit. Jesus' statement in Mk employs this motif of a disciple's fidelity, varying it through negative phrasing.

  d. The reference to the future epiphany of the Son of Man in Mk 8:38 raises the question of its timing. According to Mk 9:1 the Kingdom of God will arrive in power before the present generation has completely died. Thus a considerable span of time will elapse between the moment when these words are spoken and that event. In terms of the Elijah/Elisha Narrative, "the coming in power" corresponds to the full establishment of the LORD's sovereignty in both Samaria and Jerusalem (2 Kgs 8:28–10:28, 11:1–20), while its initiation is correlated with the preparatory act of the divinely decreed designation of Hazael (2 Kgs 8:7–15, comp. 1 Kgs 19:15–17). The time span between these events is not expressly quantified, but its length implied in related narratives.

  Since the two brief reports on the eight-year reign of Joram of Judah and of the one-year rule of his successor Ahaziah (2 Kgs 8:16–24, 25–27) intervene between the Elisha-Hazael (2 Kgs 8:7–15) and the Elisha-Jehu narratives (2 Kgs 9:1–10:30), the readers know that some nine years elapse between the two episodes. Furthermore, the overthrow of Baal was completed only with the eradication of his worship in the southern capital, which occurred seven years after Jehu's coup in Samaria. In addition, there is the earlier statement that Ahab's repentance after Jezebel's murder of Naboth will delay the end of the Omride dynasty by one generation (1 Kgs 21:27–29). On the other hand, according to Mk 9:1 the period between Jesus' appearance and the disclosure of the Kingdom in power is of the length of nearly one generation: Some of those who witnessed the martyrdom of Jesus will live to witness the Kingdom's arrival in power as signalled by Jesus' appearance from heaven as Son of Man, evidently immediately after the destruction of the Jerusalem Temple in 70 C.E. (comp. Mk 13:1–23).

6.1.4 Temple Restorations

The narration of Jesus' setting in order the affairs of the Temple
(Mk 11:15-17) as well as of the negative impact of his intervention on persons of importance (Mk 11:18) develops motifs of the
Elijah/Elisha Narrative. After King Joash had been enthroned
as divinely confirmed king in Jerusalem (2 Kgs 11:17), the local
Baal sanctuary and its priest were destroyed and guards appointed for the house of worship of Israel's God (2 Kgs 11:18).
Moreover, in 2 Kgs 12:5-17 there is described the manner in
which the divinely approbated monarch eventually makes an
end of the neglect of the maintenance of the LORD's house. He
came to know that repairs had not been carried out even though
money had been given to the clergy for that purpose by their
benefactors. So the king, in his twenty-third year, decreed that
a different arrangement was to be made: All worshippers would
have their free will offering for the Temple's upkeep deposited
in a box especially constructed and set up at the entrance of
the sanctuary for that purpose; it would be emptied from time
to time by a priest and a royal officer and the collected silver
given to the craftsmen charged with the maintenance of the holy
precinct.

This story, told at the end of the sustained narration of the
re-establishment of the LORD's sovereignty in 1 Kgs 17-2 Kgs
13, is also its climax. And it is as such that it supplies base
and plot for the evangelist's narrative of Jesus' cleansing of the
Temple at the end of the master's public activity (see also the
discussion in 2.2 above of the relation of Jesus' Temple cleansing to his baptism by John). In this framework 2 Kgs 12:5-17
also provides the motif of Jesus' warning against the greed of
the religious leaders of his time and of his commendation of the
poor widow who had put all she had into the offering box (Mk
12:38-44, comp. the discussion of her commendation by Jesus
in 5.2.7 above). Broadly speaking, the two parts of the story of
Joash's ordering the Temple affairs (2 Kgs 12:5-9/10-17) provide to Mk the narrative frame for the compositional unit 11:1-

12:44: Jesus begins by ridding the sanctuary of those who seek to derive from it personal gain (Mk 11:15–17; comp. 11:11 and 11:1–10) and concludes by commending gifts of devotion offered for it (Mk 12:41–44). In addition to the plot correspondence between 2 Kgs 12:5–17 and Mk 11:15–17, the evangelist signals the unique relation through the triple use of the technical term for the offering box of 2 Kgs 12:9–11 .

6.1.5   Visions of War

Mk 13:1–37 is set off from what precedes and follows by the identification of its restricted audience. In response to the question of Peter, James, John, and Andrew as to when the destruction of the Temple will occur and what its sign will be (Mk 13:2, 4), Jesus discourses on events of the future that bring great agony and culminate in the coming of the Son of Man and his ingathering of the elect (Mk 13:5–20, 21–27). He concludes with a call to be vigilant (Mk 13:28–37). The four disciples are the exclusive recipients of this instruction and thus enabled to decode the significance of coming wars and persecutions (Mk 13:6–13), of the setting up of "the abomination of desolation" and the ensuing sufferings (Mk 13:14–20), of the appearance of false anointed ones and pseudoprophets (Mk 13:21–23), and of the failure of sun, moon, and stars (Mk 13:24–25) as indication of the imminent epiphany of the Son of Man (Mk 13:26–27). Jesus' order to remain watchful, illustrated by two parables (Mk 13:28–29, 34–36), is directed to them (Mk 13:28–36) and, through them, to all (Mk 13:37).

Mk 13 is placed between the narration of Jesus' words and deeds (Mk 1:14–12:44) and the story of his martyrdom and vindication (Mk 14:1–16:8), separating as well as connecting the two units. However, it is not only a transitional text, but also a composition in its own right. What are its narrative motivation and the reason of its placement in its context? A similar transition text, located in a corresponding context, is found in the Elijah/Elisha Narrative. After the deeds of Elisha, which authenticate him as prophet of the LORD, have "all been told" (2 Kgs 8:4, comp. 2:13–8:6), the storytellers narrate the overthrow of apostasy and the full establishment of the LORD's sovereignty in Israel and Judah (2 Kgs 8:16–13:25). However, the narrative train does not move directly to the city of Samaria and the Kingdom of Israel. Before the ultimate confrontation in the capital(s) of Israel (and Judah) is told, a unit intervenes that narrates Elisha's journey to Damascus in order to initiate the removal of King Ben-hadad and the installation of Hazael as king over Aram (2 Kgs 8:7–15). The audience of 1 Kgs 17–2 Kgs 13 already knows through the preview in 1 Kgs 19:15–17 that this action is the first of the steps that will lead to the public and complete abolition of the worship of the foreign god (2 Kgs 8:16–13:25).

The story of 2 Kgs 8:7–15 narrates that when Elisha was approaching the Syrian capital, he was met by an embassy, led by Ben-hadad's servant Hazael. He brought forty camel loads of wealth for the prophet and was charged to inquire whether the king, afflicted with sickness, would survive. Elisha told Hazael to relay a reassuring message, even though the God of Israel "had shown" otherwise to him. When Hazael pressed Elisha for more details (?), Elisha broke into tears. In response to Hazael's question why he was weeping, Elisha said, "I know what you will do to the Israelites is evil: You will put their fortresses to the torch, slaughter their young men with the sword, bash their infants against the wall and slit open their pregnant women" (2 Kgs 8:12). To Hazael's further, deferential inquiry as to how he, "the dog" (comp. the discussion of the comparison of proselytes to little dogs in 5.1.3 above), would be able to accomplish such a great thing, Elisha answered, "The LORD has let me see you as king over Aram" (2 Kgs 8:13). Upon return to Damascus Hazael delivered Elisha's reassuring message to the monarch, but on the following day assassinated him and became king in his place.

The divine command given to Elisha's forerunner Elijah at Mount Horeb (1 Kgs 19:15–17) indicates that Hazael's claiming

his master's throne is the first of two royal overthrows, thus
leaving only that of Joram, the last of the Omride dynasty,
to be carried out. Moreover, the Elisha story emphasizes a
visionary element in that the causative form of the verb "to
see" is used twice: The LORD "has let me see ..." (2 Kgs 8:10,
13). Thus 2 Kgs 8:7–15 corresponds compositionally to Mk 13
in that the latter, like its model, serves to move the narration
from preparation to execution of the divine design.

The correlation is also evident in the evangelist's use of the
imagery of war and the sufferings it inflicts on the elect. The
coming conflict between Aram and Israel and its horrors make
the prophet weep when he sees Hazael as future king (2 Kgs
8:12). Specifically, Jesus' discourse employs two related verbal
images drawn from the model story: the evil treatment that
pregnant and nursing women will receive. While Mk does not
reproduce each gruesome detail of 2 Kgs 8:12, it has Jesus ex-
claim "woe!" over women who will be pregnant and those who
will nurse infants at the time of the coming upheaval (Mk 13:17).

6.1.6   *Preservations Unto Life*

The gospel's final section (Mk 15:40–16:8) sets forth the vindication of the martyred Jesus. Here two stories of the actions
of certain women followers of Jesus (Mk 15:40–41/15:47–16:8)
frame the narrative of the intervention by Joseph of Arimathea
after Jesus' demise (Mk 15:42–46). The women witness their
master's death and later see the place where his body is put.
After the sabbath they return but do not find the corpse in the
cave where it had been laid; they are told by a heavenly messenger that Jesus is risen and that he will go before his disciples
to Galilee where they will see him. Struck by fear they do not
tell the vision to anyone.

Two motifs of the Elijah stories provide conceptual-literary
foils for this last section of Mk: on the one hand, the notion of
the preservation of men loyal to Israel's God in a cave, secured
there by a worshipper of the LORD (1 Kgs 18:4, 13), and, on the

other, the narrative motif that the failure to locate a Man of God after a three-day search amounts to, or at least implies, the confirmation of his assumption into the celestial sphere (2 Kgs 2:15–18).

The story of the placing of Jesus' body into a rock-cut cave closed with a large stone tells of an act of courageous piety by a highly placed councilor. The request of Joseph for Jesus' body, directed to the procurator, is granted; it is evidently not construed by Pilate as belated indication of complicity with the crucified man. The cave is described as "hewn out of the rock" and secured with a large stone. Joseph's action preserves the body for burial, possible only after the sabbath, which the women's action on the first day of the week is designed to initiate.

The notion of the preservation of persons loyal to Israel's God in a cave by a highly placed worshipper of the LORD is reminiscent of one of the arguments with which King Ahab's vizier Obadiah seeks to persuade Elijah not to act in such a manner that it endangers the prophet's life. He points out that when Jezebel slaughtered the LORD's prophets, he hid a hundred of them "in a cave," supplied them with food and in this manner preserved them from certain death at the hand of the apostate queen (1 Kgs 18:4, 13). While the evangelist does not expressly refer to a cave, the notion of preservation is present, coupled with the correspondence between the high social positions of Obadiah in the Elijah story and of Joseph in the gospel passage.

On the other hand, the attestation of Jesus' rising by a celestial messenger occurs on the morning of the day after the sabbath, which in Mk 8:31, 9:31, and 10:34, though not in Mk 16:1–8, is said to occur "three days" after Jesus' crucifixion. This suggests that the evangelist's narration be read against the backdrop of the story of the fifty prophet-disciples of Jericho who insist against Elisha's wishes on a search for the disappeared Elijah. They urge Elisha to accede to their request, "lest the LORD's spirit take him and throw him on one of the mountains or into one of the valleys." The narrator continues, "they searched for three days, yet did not find him." Their inability to find the Man of God after a three-day search not only vindicates Elisha's initial refusal of their request but also serves to confirm that the Tishbite had indeed been assumed into heaven.

6.2 Narrative Sequences

The evangelist also models series of narrative units on the basis of motifs found in 1 Kgs 17–2 Kgs 13. For instance, the cluster of controversy stories in Mk 2:1–3:6, Jesus' triple elaboration of offending organs of the body in Mk 9:43–48, and, most of all, the narrative of his martyrdom in Mk 14:1–15:39 have counterparts in the scriptural model either in basic motif selection or in plot conceptualization. This section concludes the discussion of correlations between Mk's narration and 1 Kgs 17–2 Kgs 13 with the exploration of their compositional foils and in this manner returns to the question with which the inquiry began.

6.2.1 Controversy Stories

Mk 2:1–3:6 is a grouping of stories unified by the theme of "controversy between the man of God and those in secular or spiritual authority." The theme is that of Elisha's opposition to the King of Israel as told in 2 Kgs 3:13–14 (4–27). Already in its progression from Mk 1:35–45 to Mk 2:1–3:6 the gospel follows the narrative movement from 2 Kgs 2:23–25 to 2 Kgs 3:13–14. In form, the gospel's controversy stories relate to different issues under debate between Mk's Jesus and his adversaries; all come to their climax in a response of Jesus to his opponents by way of refutation (Mk 2:8–11, 17, 19–22, 25–27, 3:5; comp. Elisha's castigation of the king in 2 Kgs 3:13–14). In the actual narrative casting of the individual units the evangelist develops a variety of scriptural motifs drawn from elsewhere in 1 Kgs 17–2 Kgs 13 or in "the Prophets" at large: The healing of the paralytic (Mk 2:1–12) is based on the story of King Ahaziah's fatal fall from his roof and his ensuing apostasy in 2 Kgs 1:2–17a (see

6.1.1 above), while the call of Levi (Mk 2:14 [15–17]) has its foil in that of Elisha by Elijah in 1 Kgs 19:19–21. Two of Mk's units relate to texts outside the Elijah/Elisha Narrative: The issue of food consumption on the sabbath (Mk 2:23–28) points to David's action in an emergency as told in 1 Sam 21:1–7, and Jesus' healing of the withered hand (Mk 3:1–5) to what is told of King Jeroboam usurping priestly prerogatives in 1 Kgs 13:1–6. On the other hand, Jesus' brief discourse on fasting (Mk 2:18–20) alludes to the role of that same motif in the Naboth story (1 Kgs 21) and the parabolic sayings on the incompatibility of the new and the old (Mk 2:21–22) have as foil that very lesson as illustrated by the Elijah/Elisha Narrative in its entirety.

The five units of Mk 2:1–3:6 seek to settle controversies with those in authority in the larger community of Judaism, and do so through pronouncements made by Jesus. They relate to different claims advanced by or on behalf of the man from Nazareth: (1) His authority to forgive sins, which according to some theologians is reserved to God alone, (2) his freedom to associate and share meals with religious outcasts, behavior frowned upon by Pharisaic Scripture scholars, (3) his and his disciples' non-observance of fasting customs that are followed both by the disciples of John the Baptist and by Pharisees, (4) his and his disciples' plucking corn on the sabbath for personal consumption, an action that the Pharisees claim to be prohibited on that day of the week, and finally (5) his restoration of a withered hand on the sabbath, an action that his unnamed opponents claim not to be permitted on that day.

The framework and the theme of these units are provided by the narrative about the campaign of the three kings against the Moabite monarch in which Elisha participated (2 Kgs 3:4–27). After the prophet had been commissioned and proven his status through the performance of three miracles, he is in this story portrayed in the retinue of the Israelite king, the latter accompanied by Jehoshaphat, King of Judah, and by the King of Edom; the cause of their campaign was the rebellion of Mesha, King of Moab, against Israel after Ahab's death (comp. 2 Kgs 1:1).

On their march through the desert, the kings find themselves without water. Upon Jehoshaphat's request the only prophet of the LORD who is present, Elisha son of Shaphat, is called before the kings and an inquiry of the LORD made through him. But Elisha refuses to do so on behalf of the Israelite king: "What have I and you to do with each other? Go to the prophets of your father and the prophets of your mother!" The chastised king responds deferentially that the God of Israel seems to have brought the three kings into this situation in order to deliver them into the power of Moab. Elisha answers, "By the LORD of hosts, whom I serve, were it not that I respected the King of Judah, I would not even look at you." Then Elisha has a harp player brought and prophesies, while the musician plays, that Israel will receive water and even defeat Moab. This indeed happens, but the sacrifice of the Moabite king's first-born son on the wall of his city brings divine anger over Israel so that they have to withdraw without taking the city.

It is evidently the sharp opposition of the prophet of the LORD to the apostate king, tempered by Elisha's respect for the loyal King of Judah, that gives the thematic profile to 2 Kgs 3:4–27, which, in turn, the evangelist employs as base motif for the cluster of controversy stories in Mk 2:1–3:6.

6.2.2 Offense of Hand, Foot, and Eye

Why does Mk's Jesus, within the discourse on "offense" (Mk 9:42–50), refer to three organs of the human body (Mk 9:43–48) as instruments through which unacceptable actions are carried out? Specifically, why does he begin the series of three warnings with reference to "the hand"?

Readers who have been alerted to the role that 1 Kgs 17–2 Kgs 13 plays in the narration of the gospel wonder whether the motif of "the offending hand" is drawn from the story of Elisha's cleansing the leprosy of the Syrian commander Naaman (2 Kgs 5:15–17 [1–27]). When the Aramean is ready to return to his homeland with a load of Israelite soil in order to worship on it the God of Israel, he also anticipates that he will be compelled to carry out a duty that runs counter to his devotion to the LORD: "Only in this one regard may the LORD forgive your servant: when my master enters the temple of (his god) Rimmon in order to bow down, and he leans on my hand so that I also bow down in Rimmon's temple — when I so bow down, may the LORD forgive your servant in this matter." Elisha does not object but dismisses Naaman in peace. The Syrian proselyte is aware of the compromising situation into which his "hand" supporting his royal master places him. However, the narrator evidently considered such action pardonable.

Jesus' discourse on the offending hand is conceptually based on that motif in the Elisha story. Unlike the prophet, Jesus condemns compromising actions carried out through a person's hand; he prefers that it be cut off and in this manner free the person from the temptations of apostasy. The more radical position of the gospel also explains the addition of two like-structured strictures against the offending foot and eye (Mk 9:45–48). The tripling of the motif is noteworthy also because the Naaman story employs the (offending) verb "to bow down (in pagan worship)" three times (2 Kgs 5:18) — a numerical correspondence in compositional technique comparable to the use of numerical values as connectors (see 2.1, 2.7, 5.2.1–3 above).

6.2.3 Paradigm of Martyrdom

The composition of the sustained narration of Jesus' martyrdom (Mk 14:1–15:39) is conceptually shaped by two interacting and mutually supporting motif patterns, both found in 1 Kgs 17–2 Kgs 13. The first is that of the corresponding (third) act of the Elijah/Elisha Narrative (2 Kgs 8:16–12:17): The confrontation with the powers of apostasy in the capital(s) leading to its over-throw and the ensuing establishment of the LORD's sovereignty. The second is the narration of the one martyrdom suffered by a faithful Israelite that is told in the Elijah/Elisha Narrative: Jezebel's and her co-conspirators' murder of the falsely accused vineyard owner Naboth, the Jezreelite (1 Kgs 21:1–29, comp. 22:39–40 and 2 Kgs 9:30–37). The two scriptural strains intersect in the narration of Judas's betrayal and illustrate the truth of the lesson that the vineyard parable (Mk 12:1–12) had already spelled out.

The first and more basic pattern of composition in this part of the gospel corresponds to the sequencing of individual motifs in the third act of the Elijah/Elisha Narrative (see 3.2.1 above). There the authentication of Elisha through his words and deeds as told in the second act (2 Kgs 2:13–8:6) leads, after the transitional story (2 Kgs 8:7–15) of visions of coming upheavals (see 6.1.5 above), to the third act: the fateful encounter of the agents of Israel's God with the foreign god Baal and his royal and cultic supporters in the capitals of Israel and Judah. Not only the sequence of the major acts of the gospel's narration corresponds to the scriptural model, but also the narration of Jesus' rejection, suffering, and death correlates, though by way of inversion, to its biblical antecedent: Jehu (and Joash) advance to victory on behalf of Israel's God, but Jesus does so by way of dying a violent death, falsely accused of sedition.

The observation that Jesus does not mount a throne as newly acclaimed king but is, though innocent, put to death, points to the other motif pattern that structures Mk 14:1–15:39: The Naboth story (1 Kgs 21). Its lead theme is that of the rightful claimant of a vineyard (the token of his tribal allotment from the God of Israel), who finds himself through the intrigue of a royal figure accused of blasphemy and stoned to death by his town's collaborating elders and citizens. This narrative supplies the key to the evangelist's portrayal of Jesus' death outside Jerusalem as victim: The man from Nazareth is a martyr for the God of Israel like that Israelite of old! By the same token, as Naboth's death sealed the death warrant of the false claimants to the vineyard, King Ahab and his queen, so Jesus' death heralds a similar fate for his adversaries. To conclude, Mk 14:1–15:39 broadly follows in its sequencing of units 2 Kgs 8:25–12:22; it casts Jesus, however, not as victorious king but as one who is put to death. The following exploration will show in what manner certain motifs of the Jehu and Joash narration are inverted while those based on the Naboth story are heightened.

As indicated, the two organizing patterns intersect in passages in which Judas Iscariot is the actor. In terms of the Jehu and Joash stories he plays the role of the one among Jesus' intimates who breaks confidence (the emergence of such a figure is in the Jehu story mentioned as a possibility), leads the captors under cover of night and hidden from the public eye to his master's place of retreat, known only to the Twelve (Mk 14:10–11, 43–47, comp. 2 Kgs 9:15, 11:4–12), thus making it possible to carry out Jesus' opponents' plan to put him to death without causing a public commotion. In terms of the Naboth story, Judas' role is that of the bought "sons of Belial" who sit at table with their victim (Mk 14:17–21, comp. 1 Kgs 21:10, 13). Thus Jesus' adversaries appear in the roles both of Jehu's and Joash's foes who hold sway in the capitals (Mk 14:1, 10–11, 43–49, 53, 55–64; 15:1, 11, 31–32) and of Queen Jezebel who has Naboth murdered through treachery in which his fellow citizens are knowingly accomplices (Mk 14:2, 10–11, 43–49, 55–59).

The course of events as told in Mk 14:1–15:39 moves from the Jerusalem Temple clergy to the Roman officials involved in Jesus' execution. It begins with the plan of the chief priests and the theologians to kill Jesus and ends with the exclamation of a Roman centurion, who witnesses Jesus' death, that he was a "son of God" (Mk 14:1, 15:39). The Temple clergy pronounced the man from Nazareth liable to the death penalty but the Roman procurator remained unpersuaded of their claim (Mk 14:64, 15:14). The two immediate reactions to Jesus' death illustrate the contrast as well: On the one hand, the Temple curtain tears from top to bottom, baring the Holy of Holies and thus signifying the departure of the divine presence; on the other hand, a highly placed Gentile, seeing Jesus die, pronounces him a son of God (Mk 15:38/39). The same shift from the one people, the Judeans, to the peoples, the Gentiles, is reflected in the gospel's sequencing of the two feeding miracles (Mk 6:32–44/8:1–9) and of the two narratives of Jesus' exorcism of unclean spirits (Mk 1:23–28/7:24–30). In both cases sustenance and liberation are granted first to members of Jesus' own people, then to representatives of those not descended from Jacob-Israel. Moreover, while the Judeans are slow in accepting him, the others respond eagerly (Mk 8:1–3, 7:28, and comp. the discussion of the comparison of proselytes with "little dogs" in 5.1.3 above).

In addition to these compositional correlations, the evangelist draws freely on motifs of the Elijah/Elisha Narrative in order to suggest it as a primary scriptural backdrop. Several examples have already been discussed: Judas' kiss of betrayal (see 5.1.1 above), Jesus' last cry "with a loud voice" (5.1.6 above), and Peter's threefold denial of his master as inversion of Elisha's triple affirmation of his loyalty when the Tishbite journeys to his assumption, together with the related numerical combination "2/3" in the reference to the cock's second crow after Peter's third denial (see 2.7 above). The following exploration of five other correlations will further illustrate the narrational connection: The story of the anointing of Jesus, the narrative of the covenant meal, the passage about Jesus' solitary withdrawal, the doubling of Jesus' trial proceedings (first before the religious authorities, then before the secular authorities), and finally the narration of the Roman soldiers' mocking of Jesus.

a. The story of the anointing of Jesus' head at the supper in Bethany (Mk 14:3–9) introduces a motif that is crucial in the plot of the Elijah/Elisha Narrative: The LORD's order to anoint Jehu, son of Nimshi, as king over Israel (1 Kgs 19:15–17) was in due time followed by its execution (2 Kgs 9:1–10). Elisha, recipient of that divine order through his commissioning by Elijah, sent a prophet-disciple to Ramoth-gilead. To the surprise of Jehu and his fellow officers, the prophet-disciple carried out the act of anointing, delivered the divine-prophetic order to make an end of his master's house and thus of apostasy in Israel, and then fled in haste.

The anointing motif as found here is the basis of the evangelist's story; it is both heightened and inverted. It is heightened in that the oil is described as very expensive: It is genuine myrrh contained in an alabaster vessel that is broken during the rite. The scriptural motif is inverted in that the anointing readies Jesus not for royal office but for burial — a burial, to be sure, that never actually takes place because he rises from the dead before the burial can actually be carried out. Thus a conceptual tension is evident in the burial imagery. The intention of Jesus' women followers' to prepare their master's body for burial (Mk 16:1) shows that it is the whole body, not only the head, that is "anointed for burial" (Mk 14:8). By the same token, only the head, and not the whole body, is anointed in the rite that legitimates a new king (2 Kgs 9:3, 6, comp. 1 Sam 10:1). The tension implied in the use of the image in this narrative context identifies Jesus as the anointed one both for (eventual) royal office and for (imminent) death and burial.

b. In the story of the covenant meal (Mk 14:12–26) Judas is portrayed as sitting at table with Jesus (Mk 14:18, 20). In like manner the two villains who are ready to accuse Naboth are seated opposite their victim during the public fast that had been called at Jezebel's order (1 Kgs 21:9–10). The motif of betrayal by a table companion casts Judas into the role of "the sons of Belial," and Jesus into that of Naboth. Hence Jesus' statement that "the Son of Man goes to his fate as it is written about him" (Mk 14:21) equates his death with that of the martyr of Jezreel, points to the Naboth story as the scriptural warrant for his own fate, and thus identifies it as the scripture that "is written about him" (Mk 14:21).

On the other hand, Jesus' reference to his body and blood in relation to his imminent death introduces the covenant motif. It thus connects what is observed as a Passover rite with passages in Scripture that relate to covenant initiations or renewals. And the Elijah/Elisha Narrative expressly tells of a covenant initiation that marked the completion of the overthrow of apostasy and its royal agent in Jerusalem, Queen Athaliah: "Then Jehoiada made the covenant between the LORD, the king and the people so that they become the people belonging to the LORD"

(2 Kgs 11:17). The observance of the rite is followed by the
destruction of the implements of Baal worship, its priest and
shrine, and the appointment of guards for the LORD's Temple
(2 Kgs 11:18). In the light of this antecedent the reference to
the covenant in Mk 14:24 identifies Jesus' Passover meal as the
observance that seals the establishment of the sovereignty of Israel's God over his people through Jesus' martyrdom. Heard in
the light of 2 Kgs 11:17-18, the words of Mk's Jesus constitute
his partners present at table (or elsewhere) as the people of the
LORD and identify the related events in Jerusalem as completion
of that plot. In keeping with the scriptural foil no reference is
made to a "new" covenant nor to any periodic repetition of the
rite after Jesus' departure. Like the covenant renewal in 2 Kgs
11:17, the covenant of Mk 14:22-25 initiates a new period of
covenantal loyalty of God's people and hence is in this function
not to be repeated.

    c. The narration of Jesus' withdrawal in Gethsemane to a
place where he is alone and cannot be reached by those who
seek to capture him (Mk 14:32-42) is modeled in basic features
after the story of Elijah's withdrawal to the wilderness south
of Beersheba when threatened with death by Jezebel (1 Kgs
19:1-7). Thus the motif of Jesus' leaving behind his disciples
corresponds to that of the Tishbite's like action after reach-
ing the last Judaite town in the South. Similarly, Jesus' agony
openly expressed before God correlates with that of Elijah, and
his sadness "unto death" to that of Elijah's outcry that he has
come "to the point of death." By the same token, Jesus' fall to
the ground is reminiscent of the Tishbite's reclining and eventual lying down under a bush in exhaustion. And finally Jesus'
readiness to leave the place of temporary respite when it is time
to meet his captors corresponds to Elijah's readiness to journey
into the wilderness to Mount Horeb at God's bidding. On the
other hand, the notion of "awakening" is inverted: The Tishbite
falls asleep and needs to be awakened, while Jesus stays awake
but has to awaken his companions. Finally, also the reference to
a small container of liquid seems to connect the two texts: Elijah

at the messenger's bidding takes the water flask that strength-
ens him for the arduous trip ahead while Jesus asks God that
"this cup" might pass from him.

Evidently these motifs are freely used and combined in the
evangelist's narration. In all, Jesus is heightened in comparison
to Elijah, in keeping with the view expressed in the Transfiguration Story that in the same manner in which Elijah is the
heavenly patron for his followers, so Jesus is now the celestial
lord of his disciples (Mk 9:2–8). The evangelist's variation and
combination of biblical images, motifs, and plots into a coherent, persuasive but also new composition manifestly appeals to
the gospel's audience.

d. The trial before the high priest and the synhedrion (Mk
14:53–72) is the first of two that Jesus undergoes. The second
places him before Pilate, the Roman procurator and representative of the highest royal authority in Rome (Mk 15:1–15). In
the first trial the man from Nazareth is accused of blasphemy;
in the second of sedition. Why is the trial motif narratively
doubled in this fashion? What is its narrative motivation?

The story of the first trial begins with the reference to the
"many false witnesses" who seek to incriminate Jesus. This
term alerts readers aware of the scriptural foil to that narrative
in which "false witnesses" play a crucial role: The Naboth story
(1 Kgs 21). Its hero is accused by two such witnesses that he
has spoken against "God and king" (1 Kgs 21:10, 13). To be
sure, this is a summary formulation in keeping with the ancient
understanding that the monarch is the representative of the divine order, if not divine himself. It seems that in Mk 14:55–64
and 15:1–15, 18, 26 the (merely terminological) differentiation
between the religious and the secular authorities in 1 Kgs 21
has been heightened into a substantive doubling: Jesus' fails to
conform to both the religious and the political powers. However, this observation is in itself not conclusive evidence of the
evangelist's modeling of the story after a biblical model; after
all, the authorities recognized in Jerusalem at the time were the
Judeans' religious leaders as well as the Roman administrators.

What makes the connection likely are two details: First, it is
the accusation of "blasphemy" that is levelled by "false witnesses." Both terms are important in the Naboth story, though
the latter refers by implication, not express designation, to the
two villains' role in relation to the Jezreelite. Second, as in
the Naboth story so in the gospel the verdict is rendered by
the assembled elders and leaders (comp. 1 Kgs 21:9, 12 with Mk
14:55).

   e. Finally, the Roman soldiers' mock installation of Jesus as
"King of the Judeans" (Mk 15:16–20a) is narratively motivated
by his opponents' accusation that he is a royal pretender (Mk
15:2). Accordingly, certain details of the narration correspond
to features of King Joash's installation as King of Judah (2 Kgs
11:11–12 [1–12]), but, as might be expected, do so by way of
inversion. Thus the assembled Roman soldiers correspond to
the congregated Temple guards "around the king." The treatment of Jesus as mock king is reminiscent of Joash's endowment
with the symbols of royal office: There is the placing of the dia-
dem on the head of the Judaite king but of a crown of thorns on
that of Jesus; the delivery of Joash's scepter into his hand corresponds to the staff with which the soldiers strike the condemned
man; to Joash's acclamation as monarch corresponds the soldiers' sarcastic acclaim of Jesus as "the King of the Judeans";
to Joash's anointing seems to correspond the soldiers' spitting
at the man of sorrows; and the hand clapping in celebration of
the new king's rule correlates with the derisive genuflection of
Jesus' tormentors. In sum, both theme and details of Jesus'
mocking by the soldiers are drawn from a scriptural model and
the reversal of motifs enables the evangelist to portray Jesus as
both martyr and king (comp. Mk 15:2, 26).

Chapter 7

Mark's Hermeneutic Activity

The preceding chapters advance a thesis and seek to adduce evidence in its support: The gospel of Mark conceptualizes the appearance of Jesus, the martyr from Nazareth, in terms of a scriptural model. The paradigm is the narrative of the reestablishment of the sovereignty of the God of Israel in Israel and Judah through Elijah and Elisha, Jehu and Joash, as told in 1 Kgs 17–2 Kgs 13. Moreover, the literary execution of the evangelist's work is not only based on the plot of that narrative but also employs many of its narrative forms and thematic motifs. The following chapters are devoted to the exploration and discussion of the hermeneutic activity the result of which is the second gospel. What precisely is its nature? Are interpretive categories such as haggadic midrash and/or rhetoric imitation applicable? What religio-social settings generated the composition? How do the findings of this study relate to modern research on the gospel of Mark?

7.1 Unique Features

Before we turn to the search for analogies in Jewish-Hellenistic literature and in light of its findings seek to explore the compositional activity of Mk, a summary of characteristic features of the evangelist's mode of composition is in order. There are three. (1) While Mk presents itself as a work in its own right, it turns out to be modeled after a text unit found in the Hebrew Bible. Thus it is properly read, as it were, on two levels: on that of narration as well as on that of re-narration. (2) The literary-conceptual relationship to its model is, however, a veiled one, that is, a secret that waits to be discovered by the gospel's audience. (3) While the Elijah/Elisha Story supplies the master paradigm, narrative motifs drawn from elsewhere in the Scriptures of early Judaism are also present, indicating that the gospel's literary execution does not exclude the employment of other motifs. Finally, many of the explored features of the gospel appear only in Mk and thus set it off from the three (canonical) "gospels" together with which it has been preserved by Christian communities. Each of the characteristic features needs to be discussed more fully and, where indicated, reviewed in the light of representative samples of contemporary research (7.1.1–3). A review of Matthew's transformation of Mark's work concludes this chapter by exploring Mk's relation to the first of the canonical gospels (7.2).

7.1.1   Transparency

Readers of early Jewish and Christian writings cannot help but note more or less frequent, direct references to the Hebrew Scriptures. These may be outright quotations, introduced as such, or allusions that identify themselves as such through the adaptation of a word, phrase, or sentence found in the sacred writings. Research of these text surface connections to the Hebrew Bible is usually made the basis for the broader exploration of the relation of the early Christian scriptures to the Hebrew Bible. However, this limitation to quotations and allusions as the basis of such comparison also means that a possible transparency of early Christian compositions in their entirety to literary-conceptual models found in the Hebrew Bible does not come into view.

At this point words of caution and reorientation written some two generations ago by Paul Fiebig are appropriate:

The New Testament is still too much interpreted as if it were literally dependent on the Old Testament — in a way in which modern literary desk scholarship proceeds. As soon as one recognizes that the Old Testament made its impact in early Judaism and early Christianity not in the way in which we see it, but in the manner in which people *then* perceived it, the importance of the study of rabbinic traditions becomes clear (Fiebig 1911, 73; my translation, author's italics).

Fiebig paved the way for this probing into the manners in which early Jews and Christians appropriated Holy Writ by collecting, translating (into German), and interpreting relevant texts of the early Synagogue such as miracle stories (1911), parables (1912), and traditions that throw light on the style of the gospels (1925).

What precisely was the way in which Jews and Christians of the first century C.E. perceived and interpreted the Hebrew Bible? How did they keep its manifold heritage alive, appropriate it, and relate it to their own reflection and literary creativity? The answer is: Through the medium of "searching the Scriptures" (Jn 5:39), an activity usually and broadly defined as "midrash." Etymologically both the Greek word used in Jn 5:39 and the Hebrew term suggest the notion of "inquiry, search, exposition." The background, nature, and impact of this activity are described for instance in Leo Baeck's "The Gospel as a Document of the Jewish Faith" (originally published in German in 1938). This hermeneutic activity may be summarized as follows:

a. Baeck first shows how "midrash" emerged in early Judaism: The understanding of the Bible as a "spiritual inheritance" that is to be learned anew by each student and each generation led to

the commandment of seeking and searching in the Bible so that it might never cease really to speak and to show things. One sought and searched what the written word might proclaim and mean.... The word one read could

never be a merely written and finished word: it always
spoke, moved, and progressed. It always had something
new to say. [46]

b. Whenever Scripture spoke anew in a compelling way,
those to whom the insight had been given became teachers themselves. After all, their new yet old instruction demonstrated that
Scripture not only

related what had been once upon a time and had come and
gone, but it proclaimed something permanent and endur-
ing — something which happened long ago, but also happens again and again and is, for all the changes in place
and detail, always the same. A particular story reveals, as
it were, a grandiose drama which is performed over and
over again; the masks are changed, but the protagonists
and their opponents are always the same. [50]

c. Since the Bible was "the supreme court of all understanding and knowledge . . . , whatever happened or was said must be
understood in terms of the Bible" (51). In fact,

the words of the Bible alone could show what had really
and truly happened. Not what the eye had seen or not
seen, not what men had related or contested could furnish
a decisive answer, but only what the word of God had
proclaimed. . . . One did not only think and hope in terms
of the Scripture, but experience and knowledge, too, were
molded by it, often decisively. [51]

d. New conceptualizations of religious existence and its communities were demanded by unsettling events, notably the destruction of the central house of worship. Baeck observes that

it was in the most serious and threatening times that the
words of the Holy Scriptures were felt to be most urgent
and moving; it was then, too, that one felt the strongest
urge, if not a real compulsion, to continue the process of

creation. Disaster was in the air and many an hour suggested that a great turning point was ahead. [57]

    e. Little wonder that "the Bible itself... furnished the pattern for all these varied expressions of the poetic imagination" (59)! Thus Baeck can note that "there developed a special way of intellectual searching and finding—one might almost say, a special logic..." according to which the "Holy Scriptures were the cosmos which contained all meaning" (61). Hence,

> whatever was said or written was, in spite of all peculiarities and distinctions, presented in terms of a traditional genre, within the outlines of some ancient model. The style was fixed. [59]

Baeck's instructive description of the hermeneutic activity of early Judaism not only broadly illuminates the matrix of most of the Christian writings of the first century C.E., but also shows that the search for their transparency in relation to Holy Writ is an approach that their audiences may reasonably adopt— then as now. However, Baeck himself did not discover in the gospel's plot "the outlines of some ancient model" in the manner in which this study suggests. But then, the gospel seeks to make such recognition difficult, because it pointedly speaks of the concealment of its secret—the second feature noted above.

7.1.2   *Concealment and Disclosure*

The literary-conceptual relationship between Mk and 1 Kgs 17–2 Kgs 13 is in the second gospel not identified and shown openly and directly. Rather, it is veiled and remains a secret until it is discovered. Hence the repeated calls of Mark's Jesus that whoever "has ears, let that person hear" (Mk 4:9, 23, comp. 7:16) and, most of all, the unique reference to "the secret of the Kingdom," prefacing Jesus' solution of the parable of the sower (Mk 4:11, comp. 4:3–20). According to this hermeneutic of concealment and disclosure Mark's Jesus assures the disciples and those who are with them (adherents, it seems) that they have been initiated into that secret and thus are able to progress, though evidently only in stages, to its full recognition (comp. Mk 4:10–12 with 6:52, 8:21, 8:22–9:1, 9:9–10, 11–13, also 16:14–18). By the same token, "the outsiders" by definition lack that insight and thus can hear the parables only as words that continue to conceal the secret. Two observations about this Markan watchword are in order.

a. The notion of "the secret" has occupied Mk's interpreters ever since 1901 when William Wrede published his monograph on "the messianic secret" in the gospels, specifically in Mk. There he argued that Jesus' repeated orders to keep his messianic status secret was the literary-conceptual instrument of the evangelist through which early Christian faith in Jesus as messiah was reconciled to the non-messianic life of "the historical Jesus."

Two recent monographs illustrate the nature of the ensuing discussions. On the one hand, Theodore Weeden's *Mark — Traditions in Conflict* (1971) shifted the discussion from the messianic secret to that of christological misunderstanding. He sought to show that Jesus' teaching in the second part of the gospel (Mk 8–16) rejects and replaces his portrayal as a miracle worker that dominates the first part (Mk 1–7). Weeden bases his argument on the disciples' progression from failure to understand Jesus to, first, misconception and, finally, to rejection of their master and their own flight.

On the other hand, Madeleine Boucher's literary study *The Mysterious Parable* (1977) broadens Weeden's notion of the messianic secret to that of the parabolic secret pervading the gospel in its entirety but especially evident in the parables. She notes that the evangelist has "taken what is essential to the parable, the double meaning effect, and made it the starting point of a theological theme concerning the audience's resistance to hearing the word" (83). In conclusion she observes that the double meaning effect refers "to a parallel spiritual reality ... and it is this indirect or second level of meaning which is of import" (85).

b. The understanding of Mark's hermeneutic of concealment

and disclosure is furthered by Daniel Patte's monograph, *Early Jewish Hermeneutic in Palestine* (1975). There his discussion of "broad Biblical patterns" that serve to structure post-biblical, specifically apocalyptic compositions (159–176) is instructive.

(1) Patte first shows that the use of such patterns is the manner in which "the liturgy was structured by what was considered in Apocalyptic Judaism as being key Biblical texts (the Ten Commandments, the three texts of the Shema and the Priestly Blessings)." He observes that "in the same way the Apocalyptic texts were structured by . . . key Biblical texts (although these were only alluded to rather than recited)" (169). Patte for instance shows how the pattern "evil times now — God's intervention soon — judgment of sinners — rejoicing of the righteous then," found already in the Noah story (Gen 6–9), was employed by some authors to structure their work, notably in Ps Sol 17.

(2) Patte emphasizes that this use of Scripture to structure a composition was always combined with "other uses of Scripture" (171). One of these usages is "the anthological use" (172). Here phrases drawn from the Hebrew Bible at large are employed to formulate the apocalyptic teaching in its details. Through an analysis of Ps Sol 17 he shows how loosely Scripture is here used: "We could even say that it is not properly speaking a use of Scripture: the anthological style is relatively weak" (175). In other words, "here . . . Scripture is used as a mere language" (172). Patte further discusses how events contemporary with the writers play a crucial role in the emergence of their work: "The Biblical texts and phrases were brought together in a theme which these events suggested" (172). He summarily characterizes such apocalyptic writing in this manner:

> Thus here two poles are kept in tension: on the one hand we have Scripture, represented by the broad Biblical pattern and the weak anthological style, and on the other hand we have the events of the author's time. The Psalm is the product of this "revelatory" tension: it presents the

ultimate meaning which the author discovered in his contemporary history. [175]

This revelatory tension seems to be also the matrix of Mark's
work: On the one hand, there were the events of Jesus' life,
especially his martyrdom, followed a generation later by the
destruction of the Temple in Jerusalem. On the other hand,
there was the canon of the Hebrew Scriptures, offering in the
Elijah/Elisha Narrative "a broad biblical pattern" of the re-
establishment of the LORD's sovereignty in Israel and Judah
in the face of apostasy; it thus stood ready to offer itself as
a possible conceptual model of Jesus' appearance as follower
of John the Baptist and as martyr in Jerusalem, and that a
generation before the events of 70 C.E.

Before this issue is pursued further, a reference to several
examples serves to illustrate the point made by Patte. For instance, post-biblical sages saw in the Song of Songs a broad biblical pattern that is able to supply a paradigmatic framework
for Israel's relationship to its God and that, interpreted thus,
is capable of support through many quotations from "the Law
and the Prophets" — a procedure that illustrates the two uses
of Scripture identified by Patte (see also Heinemann 137). Or,
the Similitudes of 1 Enoch are, as Suter shows, composed by using Is 24–27 as the structuring biblical pattern that supplies the
lead-theme and motifs in detail. Similarly, the Book of Daniel
is structured according to a scriptural pattern, that of the sequence "authentication of the apocalyptic seer by tests — visions
of the apocalyptic seer" (Dan 1–6/7–12), a pattern drawn from
the Joseph Story (comp. esp. Gen 39–41).

On the other hand, a passage in *Ant* XX 167–168 also illustrates the function of scriptural paradigms. Josephus writes
that in the time of the procurator Felix (52–59 C.E.) "imposters
and deceivers called upon the mob to follow them into the
desert. For they said that they would show them unmistak-
able marvels and signs that would be wrought in harmony with
God's design." The last phrase evidently refers to an expecta-

tion model that served to provide a conceptual framework according to which "signs and marvels" are interpreted as proofs of the progressing realization of the expected scenario and so prompt the people to follow its advocates. Finally, in the light of this passage from *Ant,* the gospel's identification of Joseph of Arimathea as a person "who was also himself looking for the Kingdom of God" (Mk 15:43) seems to suggest that he preserved Jesus' body in a cave (see 6.1.6 above) over the sabbath because he espoused the same expectation model as the evangelist. Thus his placement of the body in a cave was according to his scriptural expectation model not a necessary, temporal measure in order to make due burial possible, but a preservation unto life.

These examples show that broad biblical patterns that structure new compositions are not expressly identified as such but suggested to the audience by way of allusion (Patte 169). This agrees with the evidence that the second gospel presents. For instance, it refers at the beginning, in the middle, and at the end to Elijah (Mk 1:6, 9:9–10, 15:35–36), thus alerting its audience to a comprehensive correspondence to this scriptural figure and hence to the sustained narrative in which he plays a central role.

Mark's hermeneutic of concealment and disclosure, while in narrative substance unique and characteristic of the second gospel, is in its formal features paralleled in early Jewish and Christian writings, such as the Book of Daniel, the Dead Sea Scrolls, and the Letters of Paul. A review of various aspects of this phenomenon may illustrate the observation.

a. There is first the notion that God's plan is a secret that is made known only by special revelation to the initiated and that remains hidden to outsiders (Mk 4:10–12, comp. Dan 9:22, 2:18–19, 1QpHab VII 1–5, and Rom 11:25–26). Thus it can be held that only persons who have been given "ears to hear" and "eyes to see" are able to understand the mystery, while the others are of hardened heart (Mk 4:23, 6:52, 7:16, 8:18, comp. Dan 12:8–10, CD II 14–16, 2 Cor 3:14b–16). Specifically, it is the gift of the spirit that singles persons out to be carriers of this hidden knowledge (Mk 1:10, 13:10; also 1:18, 3:29, 8:12, 14:38; comp. Dan 4:5, 6:15, 5:11–14, 1QH XII 11–13, Rom 8:16, 26, 1 Cor 12:3).

b. The full insight into the divine secrets mediated through the privileged seer may come to the recipients in stages: at first they see only dimly, but eventually fully and clearly (Mk 8:14–21, 22–26, comp. Dan 1:17–21, 2:46–47, CD I 8–10, 10–13, 1 Cor 13:12). In consequence, the full insight granted to the initiated is then set forth in words and deeds that are acclaimed as "new" (Mk 1:27, 2:21–22; comp. Dan 9:22–23, 1QH XI 12–13, 2 Cor 5:17).

c. The progress in the realization of the secret, that is, of the coming of God's rule, is gauged through the observation of signs that follow each other; the initiated are in advance instructed concerning them and thus able to recognize and interpret them (Mk 13:4, 22, 8:11–13; comp. Dan 3:32–33, 6:28, 1QS X 5, 1 Cor 1:22, 14:22). Great tribulations precede or accompany the overthrow of the old order; they can be described in a variety of ways (Mk 13:7–25; comp. Dan 12:1, 1QS IV 12–13, 1 Cor 15:24–26, 54–55). By the same token, the annihilation of the forces of apostasy as well as the appearance of the blessings of the new order are portrayed in different modes (Mk 13:27, comp. Dan 12:2b–3, 1QS IV 7–12, 1 Thes 4:16–17, 5:3, 1 Cor 15:51–57). Those who remain faithful to the end will, as a remnant, enter the new order (Mk 13:27; comp. Dan 12:1, 10:12, CD I 4–5, 1QH VI 7–8, 1 Thes 4:13–18).

d. The persons specially enlightened by God through the spirit are held in high esteem and identified with titles of honor due those who "in authority" instruct others. Thus they are the ones "who have insight" (Dan 12:3), "the righteous teacher" (CD I 11, 1QpHab VII 4–5) or "the one who transmits understanding to others" (1QS III 13, VIII 12); in the second gospel that person is portrayed as recipient of the spirit and, accordingly, as a teacher "in power" (Mk 1:9–11, 27, 14:14; comp. 4:38, 5:35, 9:17, 38, 10:17, 35, 12:14, 19, 32, 13:1).

These observations in relation to the notion of "the secret" demonstrate that the gospel's hermeneutic of concealment and disclosure readily aligns itself with analogous features in comparable early Jewish and Christian writing. They illustrate the conceptual freedom and motif variety that characterize these compositions, evident also in their use of patterns and motifs that stem from elsewhere in the Scriptures or are found in the cultural setting of the evangelist. Hence a discussion of the relation of what has emerged as the (or a) master paradigm to other models that may be discerned in or have been claimed for the second gospel is in order.

7.1.3 Model and Models

The discussion of the cluster of controversy stories (Mk 2:1–3:6; see 6.2.1 above) shows that the gospel employs narrative motifs not only from the Elijah/Elisha Narrative but also from elsewhere in the Hebrew Scriptures. This is one of several indications that the evangelist employs the model provided by 1 Kgs 17–2 Kgs 13 as master paradigm in order to accommodate within it other models. Thus a brief identification and discussion of the latter is indicated.

Patterns and motifs may be drawn from texts of the Hebrew Bible outside the Elijah/Elisha Narrative or, it seems, from extra-scriptural sources. Moreover, they may primarily relate to the gospel in its entirety, its macrostructure, or more to its constituent smaller text units, its microstructures. In either case, we may expect to discover juxtaposition or interaction of motifs and patterns. Is not the Hellenistic civilization eminently characterized by synthesis and interpenetration of the distinct traditions it inherited?

Vernon K. Robbins's monograph *Jesus the Teacher: A Socio-Rhetorical Interpretation of Mark* (1984) makes a persuasive case for this kind of interaction:

> The gospel of Mark represents a biographical account produced in a cultural setting that took Jewish prophetic

traditions into an intellectual environment engaged in
the dynamics of Greco-Roman *paideia*.... The document
was dominated by the cycle of relationships that emerges
around a teacher who gathers disciple-companions; com-
municates and manifests his system of thought and action
in their presence; and accepts arrest, trial, and death because he presents an alternative system of thought and
action.... [167]

While Robbins's argumentation is based on an analysis of Mark
in the light of Xenophon's *Memorabilia* and Philostratus' *Life of
Appolonius of Tyana*, it also notes and briefly discusses the shaping force of scriptural traditions concerning Abraham, Moses,
Elijah, Elisha, and Jeremiah for the second gospel. He shows
in detail how the combination of repetitive, conventional, and
progressive forms molds the work as a whole into a composition
that, in Talbert's words, "a Hellenistic reader ... would have understood ... in much the same terms as he would have used in
interpreting Laertius' Life of Empedocles. Here is a *theios aner*
about whom the claim is made that he became an immortal at
the end of his career" (42, quoted by Robbins 196).

Robbins repeatedly emphasizes and in fact begins his study
with the observation that "the authors of the NT gospels wrote
documents that exhibit a fascinating intermingling of Jewish
and Greco-Roman patterns of thought and action" (2, comp.
69–76, 113–119). Indeed, mutual penetration of scriptural and
non-scriptural, "Jewish" and "Hellenistic" elements, although
varying in kind and degree from author to author, characterizes most of early Judaism. It is difficult to say which element
dominates in a given case because authors may have sought
to balance or merge their various traditions. While our analysis limits itself to the demonstration that the Elijah/Elisha
Narrative is the scriptural master paradigm of Mk, it is open
to the claim that literary structuring in accord with a Greco-
Roman teacher-disciple relationship is at work as well. The
Elijah/Elisha Narrative may indeed be read and appropriated

as teacher-disciple stories by an audience familiar with such a socio-literary pattern. In other words, our inquiry aligns itself with that of Robbins in that it attempts to show how Jewish, that is, "scriptural" tradition asserts itself, as it were from the inside, within Mark's Roman-Hellenistic setting and literary execution. The detailed exploration of this "intermingling" in the individual text units cannot be pursued in this monograph but must be left to a commentary on the second gospel.

Aside from Robbins's interpretation of the gospel's structure in the light of Greco-Roman evidence, three explorations of the gospel's composition in the light of the Hebrew Scriptures need to be reviewed: Hartmann's and Brown's analyses of the correspondence of sequences of Jesus' miracles to the series of great deeds accomplished by Elisha, Bowman's thesis that the gospel is a "new Christian Jewish Passover Haggadah," and Derrett's monograph on the scriptural bases of Mk.

a. Correspondences between the series of miracles in Mk 4:35–8:10 and the sequence of Elisha's deeds of power are discussed in Hartmann's monograph on the structure of the gospel (1936). His study is guided by the desire to recover the preaching of Peter. In this connection he shows (147–151) that the sequencing of Jesus' miracles is, with one exception, the same as that of Elisha's miracles in 2 Kgs 2–7. Brown's essay on "Jesus and Elisha" (1971) further explores Hartmann's observations and expands the investigation to other correspondences between Old Testament texts relating to prophets, notably Jeremiah, and gospel texts. He concludes that "the gospel as a literary form is undoubtedly a *novum* but it is not without partial antecedents in the histories of the prophets of Israel" (99; comp. Achtemeier's related observations: 1970, 291; 1972, 202–205, which, however, are made to serve redaction-critical conclusions). Evidently, the investigations of these scholars are based on some of the observations that underlie our study and their conclusions support in a limited way our thesis.

b. The interpretation of Mk as "the new Christian Jewish Passover Haggadah" by John Bowman (1965) argues, in relation to Mk, the thesis that "the form of not only the individual incidents of the Life and Ministry (of Jesus) is determined by Midrash on selected Old Testament passages, but the form of the whole Gospel itself [is] determined by such" (xiii). He concludes that the Passover Haggadah with all its diversity but underlying unity provided the pattern not merely for the Last Supper, but for the whole of Mark's Gospel form (xiv).

Bowman's analysis is methodologically akin to the one pursued in this study because he attempts to show that the gospel in its entirety is shaped by an inherited conceptual-literary model. Evidently, his postulated paradigm is quite another than the one proposed in this study. However, a sustained controversy with a methodologically similar but in substance different analysis is not undertaken here, because it would transform this study into a polemical treatise. Suffice it to observe concerning Bowman's main thesis that the Passover motif is indeed present in Mk, but only in 14:12–26. There it is pointedly not portrayed as such — thus there is no mention of the Passover meal — but serves as the setting for the sealing of the establishment of God's rule through a covenant, alluding to its counterpart at the end of the third act of the Elijah/Elisha Narrative: the covenant administered by Priest Jehoiada (2 Kgs 11:17). Thus the covenant motif in Mk 14:22–26 is dominant, and as such correlates the climax of Jesus' words and deeds in Mk with the success of those of the agents of the LORD as told in the Elijah/Elisha Narrative.

c. A comprehensive discussion of the origins of the second gospel has recently been offered by J. Duncan M. Derrett in his *The Making of Mark: The Scriptural Bases of the Earliest Gospel* (1985). Derrett's method of study is close to the one adopted here, but leads him to the identification of a much more broadly defined, different scriptural "base" of the second gospel. Thus a more extensive discussion of his work is in order.

Derrett's Preface and Introduction (1–8, 9–45) lay out his methodological assumptions. Observing that the early Christians "assumed that the Old Testament was holy, and that it was an authentic source for enlightenment when the meagre traditions about Jesus turned out to be obscure and inadequate" (16), he argues that the second evangelist

> selected his material and arranged it so that it might tell the story of Jesus as parallel to, and step by step analogous with, the story of Moses and Joshua. Analogous, but also to the disadvantage of the latter. The similarities are brought out, but never obtrusively. No piece of his material is hammered until it directly recalls the model, yet the model is never lost sight of. Each section of Mark is a preacher's prompt; the whole a homiletic mnemonic continuum. [24]

Specifically Derrett seeks to show that

> Mark 1–12 is written to parallel, and to comment upon, Exodus, Numbers and Joshua, concentrating on details in broad sequence, but ignoring episodes and material which, as they stand, are repugnant to the gospel.... Genesis and Deuteronomy loom in the background, taken more or less for granted. Brackets of relevance stretch across different amounts of the gospel. The whole story, 1–16, is illustrated by Lamentations, and a considerable area by Canticles. A somewhat more restricted area attaches to 1 Samuel. Still more restricted is the use of Isaiah, particularly Is 53, and of Psalms, particularly Ps 22. [24]

These lengthy quotations summarize both Derrett's approach and his findings. In short, "a Christian Kabbala existed under the surface of Mark..." (35). Thus the gospel's "style is only superficially popular, and... presupposes a skilled decoding by a trained expert in scripture" (37).

If Derrett's investigation is based on premises evidently close to mine, why does he come to substantially different results? Does such discrepancy not compromise the method of analysis advocated by both of us? Not necessarily — after all, almost any method of analysis can produce diverging, if not contradictory, results.

To begin with, I start with the limited, but clear evidence of specific words, phrases, numbers, names, and narrative motifs that singly and together connect Mk to one scriptural narrative in a unique manner (see chapter 2 above). The cumulation of the evidence discussed in the light of that unique correlation between Mk and 1 Kgs 17–2 Kgs 13 (see chapters 3–6 above) then compels me to describe the characteristic features of the hermeneutic activity I observe (7.1) and to search for analogies in early Jewish literature (see 8 below). Derrett, on the other hand, begins with a full and documented description of the interpretive, sermonic activity of early Judaism in relation to its Holy Writ, and then proceeds to fit the second gospel, unit by text unit, into this framework by searching for parallel motifs.

Secondly, whether one finds Derrett's evidence or mine to be stronger and hence more persuasive, the Hellenistic intermingling of traditions and patterns, discussed already, may be expected to be present in an early Christian composition on various levels. Thus, while a master plot may be derived from a clearly circumscribed, conceptually and narratively profiled portion of the Scriptures such as the Elijah/Elisha Narrative, the actual execution in details may range beyond that conceptual model and incorporate patterns and motifs from elsewhere within — or outside of — Scripture. The most comprehensive, but also the most mechanical use of the entirety of Holy Writ by Mk is evident in the range of prooftexts actually quoted (see the following excursus, 7.1.4). Prooftexts serve to legitimate the new composition through the demonstration of its probability on the basis of the official canon of holy writings. In turn, the Hebrew Bible thus appears as the most comprehensive, scriptural horizon into which the gospel places itself.

Thirdly, a plot and cast transparency of one narrative in relation to another can already be discerned within the Hebrew Bible. Thus the Elijah/Elisha Narrative evokes through its basic features the Moses/Joshua narration: There is first a general correspondence in the succession motif through which two lead figures are related to each other (1 Kgs 19:16b/Num 27:18–23), then specifically a correlation in the motif of the reception of divine directives by the first of each leader pair on the holy mountain (Elijah: 1 Kgs 19:8–18 /Moses: Ex 24:12–34:35). Moreover, Elisha passes the Jordan on dry foot like Joshua (2 Kgs 2:13–14/Jos 3:14–17) in order to begin the execution of his mission to overthrow the foreign god and his devotees (2 Kgs 9:1–10:18; 11:1–20/Jos 10:40–42); eventually the establishment of the sovereignty of Israel's God in the land of promise is sealed in both narrations by the making of a covenant (2 Kgs 10:28, 11:17–18/Jos 23:1–14:28).

It is beyond the scope of this study to probe in detail Derrett's argumentation in the light of this relation of the Elijah/Elisha Narrative to that of Moses and Joshua in Num–Jos. Suffice it to note that the identification of motif correspondence "twice removed" (in the context of this study) is persuasive to the extent to which it is based on correlated motifs the wording of which suggests correspondence. Thus Mark's description of John the Baptist in 1:6 alludes clearly to that of Elijah in 2 Kgs 1:8 (comp. Mk 9:9–11), and the evangelist's implicit counting of Jesus' miracles up to and including the healing of the deafmute in 7:31–37 demands a counting of Elisha's deeds of power in 2 Kgs 2–13. In sum, the various items of evidence adduced in support of the thesis advanced in this study are clearer, more direct, and more mutually supportive than the evidence that Derrett offers. By the same token, the transparency of 1 Kgs 17–2 Kgs 13 toward the Moses/Joshua traditions must be considered in the evaluation of Derrett's hypothesis.

7.1.4   Excursus: Prooftexts in Mark

The first two prooftexts of the gospel, expressly identified as such, are combined into one unit and alert the audience to the scriptural affirmation of the coming of a divinely sent harbinger of God's great intervention. The evangelist accomplishes this by juxtaposing a text from "the Law" with one from "the Prophets" and by introducing them (so in most ancient manuscripts) "as

written in Isaiah the Prophet" (Mk 1:2–3). Its attribution to
Isaiah only may illustrate the evangelist's notion of a unity expressed in the narrative continuity of "the Law and the Prophets," according to which the latter (a prophetic text) interprets
(and hence contains within itself) the text from "the Law" on
which it is based.

The practice of accompanying and supporting the gospel's
portrayal of Jesus' mission with prooftexts is evident throughout
its narration. They are more or less equally drawn from each of
the three parts of the Hebrew Canon, as the following selective
listing illustrates.

The Law	Gen 1:27, 2:24	Mk 10:16
	Ex 3:6	Mk 12:26
	Lev 19:18	Mk 12:31
	Num 27:16	Mk 6:34
	Dt 6:5	Mk 12:30
The Prophets	Jos 22:5	Mk 12:30–33
	1 Sam 15:22	Mk 12:33
	Is 6:9–10	Mk 4:12
	Jer 1:11	Mk 11:17
	Ezek 17:23, 31:6	Mk 4:32
	Hos 6:6	Mk 12:7
	Jon 1:4–5	Mk 4:37–38
	Zech 9:9	Mk 11:2
The Writings	Ps 22:2	Mk 15:34
	Ps 11:25–26	Mk 11:9
	Dan 7:13	Mk 13:26

It is noteworthy that no prooftext is drawn from 1 Kgs 17–2 Kgs
13! Occasionally the quotation (or near quotation) of a word or a
short phrase from the Elijah/Elisha Narrative, not introduced as
a prooftext, serves to suggest the kind of motif correspondence
that makes Mk transparent toward its model (see the discussion
especially in 3.1–3.2). At any rate, the scriptural-canonical quality of Mk in its narrative surface is ensured through the pres-

ence of prooftexts from the Hebrew Scriptures at large. The Elijah/Elisha Narrative is, as it were, the gospel's functional canon, while "the Law, the Prophets, and the Writings" are its formal canon.

7.2 Matthew's Transformation of Mark

However much Mk's features discussed so far are singular and characteristic of the second gospel, Mt as well as Lk exhibit broadly the same compositional model. This structural correspondence creates the phenomenon known as "the synoptic gospel." It aligns the first three compositions of the New Testament and sets them off from the evidently differently conceived and executed fourth gospel. On the other hand, Mt and Lk contain texts without parallel in Mk; moreover, they formulate many parallels differently.

a. The following comparison of some seven features that are Markan in cast and formulation, with their counterparts in Mt, one of the other two synoptic gospels, illustrates how the first gospel transforms the scriptural model as used in the second gospel. Thus the comparison not only throws light on the specifically Matthean perspective but also, taken with some broader comparisons and observations that it prompts, functions as a test of the hypothesis advanced in this study.

(1) The characterization of what Jesus brings as "a new teaching in power" (Mk 1:27, comp. 1:22) has no parallel in Mt. By contrast, the first gospel is at pains to describe the teaching offered by one who is discipled to the Kingdom of the Heavens as made up of what is "old" and of what is "new" (Mt 13:52, comp. the prooftext Songs 7:14). While Mt nowhere expressly identifies Jesus' teaching in this manner, it characterizes the nature of desirable instruction as both old and new, while Mk pointedly describes Jesus' teaching purely and simply as "new."

(2) Mk has the people respond after Jesus' healing of the deaf-mute with the pronouncement that "he has done all things well" (Mk 7:31–37). This formulation signals to Mk's audience

that with this deed of power Jesus measures up, quantitatively as well as qualitatively, to the standard set by Elisha (see 2.1 above). While Mt offers a comparable motif unit, it does not include the crucial statement of Mk 7:37. Its absence evidently indicates that the first gospel does not wish to emphasize that Jesus is directly to be measured by this numerical standard that the Elijah/Elisha Narrative may be taken to supply.

(3) According to Mk the disciples do not understand Jesus' warning about the leaven of the Pharisees and of the Herodians nor his rehearsal of two aspects of the two feeding stories (Mk 8:14–21, comp. 6:32–44, 51, and 8:1–9). The progressive-climactic character of the successive miracles is important for the second gospel (see 2.6 above); it corresponds to Jesus' move toward the inclusion of proselytes, of "Gentiles," into the community of his followers. Mt's parallel, on the other hand, is concerned with Jesus' relation to Pharisees and Sadducees (Mt 16:5–12) and does not lead to the telling question of Jesus, "Do you still not understand?" (Mk 8:21)

(4) While Mk's Jesus refers to "the secret of the Kingdom of God" (Mk 4:11), Mt speaks in the corresponding text unit of "the secrets of the Kingdom of the Heavens" (Mt 13:11). Mt employs the plural where Mk offers the singular. For the second evangelist "the secret" is the establishment of God's sovereignty according to the scenario laid out in the Elijah/Elisha Narrative (see 2.4 above), while Mt evidently does not wish that biblical text unit to be taken as the one and only model of the coming of God's rule. In other words, the first gospel portrays the actualization of the Kingdom of the Heavens through Jesus' mission according to more than one paradigm.

(5) When Jesus is asked by the Temple clergy in whose authority he cleanses the sanctuary (Mk 11:27–33, comp. 11: 15–17), he answers with a counter question. Since his challengers are not willing to answer it, neither does he give account of his authority. These passages imply that John's commissioning of Jesus and the Baptist's subsequent arrest trigger the chain of events that eventually leads to Jesus' confrontation with the

powers in the capital, and do so in keeping with the blueprint that the Elijah/Elisha Narrative supplies (see 2.2 above). While Mt 21:33–37 essentially parallels its Markan counterpart, the first gospel elsewhere shows that it does not consider the arrest of John the necessary and exclusive condition for Jesus' public appearance as proclaimer of the Kingdom. On the contrary, both John and Jesus proclaim the same message of the same Kingdom (Mt 3:1–2, 4–17), and do so simultaneously. The scripturally ordained sequence "Elijah–Elisha" is in Mk more consistently followed than in Mt. By the same token, the first gospel expressly makes the equation of John with Elijah an optional one (Mt 11:14, comp. Mk 9:11–13).

(6) Mk uses the term "the good news" or "the gospel" in order to characterize Jesus' words and deeds insofar as they call the hearers to change their minds and to adopt the expectation model that informs them (Mk 1:14–15). Simon and Andrew, James and John are the four men who, like the four lepers of the Elisha story of the miraculous lifting of Samaria's siege (see 5.2.2 above), become the first bearers of the good news (Mk 1:16–20, comp. 13:3–36). Moreover, Mk uses the word "the gospel" in order to describe summarily the preaching of Jesus' words and deeds to all the nations (Mk 13:10, comp. 8:38, 14:9). Also Mt uses the term in this manner but, unlike the second gospel, does not attach the call "to believe the gospel" to the summary of John's and Jesus' preaching (see Mt 3:2, 4:17). On the other hand, Mt has Jesus twice teach in synagogues and proclaim "the gospel of the Kingdom" (Mt 4:23, 9:35). In short, Mk lets the scriptural foil of 2 Kgs 2:9 (3–12) appear behind its wording, while Mt does not.

(7) A comparison of the transfiguration stories (Mk 9:2–10, Mt 17:1–9) shows that for Mt Moses is the lead figure, while for Mk it is Elijah. Moreover, the second evangelist seeks to dissociate Jesus from the two heavenly figures, while Mt seeks to associate the man from Nazareth with Moses and Elijah. On the other hand, the similarity in plot and most narrative details shows that both evangelists follow a story pattern that

presents Jesus as heavenly patron of his followers in the manner in which 2 Kgs 6:15b–17 (8–23) portrays Elisha: To Elisha's servant his master is shown in a vision surrounded by fiery chariotry, thus ranked with Elijah, and assuring him of celestial protection (comp. 4.2.3 above).

These comparisons show that Mt follows the same scriptural paradigm as Mk, that is, 1 Kgs 17–2 Kgs 13. By the same token, the first gospel differs from the second in important points.

b. A more broadly based review of the differences leads to the identification of several ways in which Mt transforms Mk: The first gospel emphasizes the continuity of Jesus' mission with "the Law and the Prophets" (see Mt 5:17), evident in the many "fulfilment" quotations (e.g., Mt 1:22), or in the commendation of the teaching (though not the practice) of the theologians who "sit in Moses' seat" (Mt 23:1). Thus Mt implies that there are more scriptural models than the one adopted by Mk, and points specifically to "the Law" made up of five sections (comp. the five teaching discourses of Matthew's Jesus: Mt 5–7, 10, 13, 18, 23–24); by the same token, the references to "the sign of Jonah" (Mt 16:1–4/Jon) and to the coming of the great flood (Mt 24:37–41/Gen 6:11–13) pointedly relate to scriptural texts outside the Elijah/Elisha Narrative.

Moreover, the first gospel stresses that Jesus is sent "only to the lost sheep of the house of Israel" (Mt 10:6, 15:24) — a restriction overcome not before the risen Jesus sends his disciples out into the world at large (Mt 28:18–20). On the other hand, the second gospel is concerned with the inclusion of proselytes into the community of Jesus' followers through Jesus' words and deeds, as the progression from the feeding of the 5,000 to that of the 4,000 indicates (comp. Mk 6:32–44 with 8:1–9 and then with 8:14–21; to be sure, Mt also contains the two feeding stories, evidently understanding them as preview of the *future* inclusiveness of Jesus' mission). By the same token, Mk thinks of Jesus' followers as a community constituted by their insight into the secret of the Kingdom, while Mt emphasizes obedience to God's will as constituting the church.

Finally, several passages in Mt oppose positions set forth in Mk. Thus the warning of Matthew's Jesus against false prophets (Mt 7:15) and the reference to "men of violence" who "since the days of John the Baptist until now do violence to the Kingdom of the Heavens" (Mt 11:12) are evidently directed against adversaries. On the other hand, Mt's commendation of "the poor in spirit, the humble, the merciful, the peacemakers" (Mt 5:3, 5, 7, 9) and the invitation to all who "labor and are heavy laden," extended by a meek master whose "yoke is easy" (Mt 11:28–30), are characteristic of Mt's perspective and possibly opposed to the admissibility of violence that the Elijah/Elisha Narrative, taken as exclusive model of Jesus' mission, may be taken to suggest.

c. To summarize, Mt is evidently based on the same literary-conceptual paradigm as Mk, but transforms and expands it. The first gospel makes Jesus' appearance more fully continuous with the canonical history of Israel and expands it so as to include five instructional discourses given by Jesus. The church, which during Jesus' terrestrial presence is constituted only by the faithful from the House of Israel, will after his rising also welcome proselytes from the descendants of Noah. The community of Jesus' followers is constituted by their more perfect obedience to the divine will as entrusted to Israel by Moses and secondarily by its insight into "the secrets of the Kingdom of the Heavens." In consequence, the narration of Jesus' appearance serves as framework for a more excellent observance of "the Law of Moses." The placement of Mt before Mk in the emerging Christian canon thus also comes to supply the ethical perspective in which Mk is to be read.

Chapter 8

Literary Analogies

The review of Mark's unique features shows that most have counterparts in early Jewish and Christian literature and hence must be seen as part of the setting in which Mk arose. Thus Baeck's perceptive description of the hermeneutic activity of early Judaism points to the transparency of new compositions in relation to already existing models and styles, notably those contained in the Scriptures (7.1.1), while Patte shows how broad biblical patterns structure subsequent literary creations (7.1.2). Moreover, patterns and motifs may be combined in order to create works that manifest the "intermingling" (Robbins) of inherited traditions that is characteristic of Hellenistic literature (7.1.3). While the distribution of prooftexts over the surface of a new composition identifies its formal canon of literature (7.1.4), the recognition of literary-conceptual paradigms structuring the work not only suggests its functional canon but also explains its unique compositional features. And it is the specific literary profile of a work such as Mk that, in the ongoing reflection of early Christian groups and individuals, comes to represent a portrayal of Jesus' mission that, as Matthew's transformation of Mark shows, is both emulated and revised (7.2).

These considerations, however, merely provide the setting for the search for the specific hermeneutic activity that created the second gospel. Do early Judaism and the Hellenistic world of the first centuries C.E. offer analogies? Apart from Lk(-Acts) and Jn, the two New Testament gospels not discussed in this study, two bodies of literature need to be considered because they arise from hermeneutic activities reminiscent of those that generated the second gospel: haggadic midrash and rhetorical imitation. The first is found in Jewish-Hellenistic literature of the first centuries C.E. while the second is similarly attested in this period. Since both are based on inherited literary tradition, appropriating and transmitting it, their exploration may be expected to throw light on the hermeneutical activity that produced Mk. For both, summary descriptions, in one case with direct reference to biblical interpretation, are available and offer a convenient basis for their review and discussion in relation to the hypothesis advanced in this study.

8.1   Haggadic Midrash

Heinemann's work *The Ways of Haggada* (Hebrew; 1970) is based on the wide range, in subject matter and time, of post-biblical narrative literature on biblical themes, texts, and institutions. Thus the typology that he presents cannot be used to describe adequately the hermeneutical activity within Judaism in any one of the centuries that it covers. By the same token, it does illustrate broadly the interpretive creativity that may be assumed to be at work certainly as soon as the literarily fixed canon of the Hebrew Bible had emerged. Thus Heinemann's monograph probes extensively and systematically what Baeck's shorter presentation (see 7.1.1 above) discusses summarily.

a. Heinemann reminds biblical scholars of the need to adopt the perspective of ancient audiences of the Bible. They were not only familiar with individual passages and formulations found in the Scriptures, but also internalized compositional patterns as well as narrative plots. The Bible was "not written to be read all at once, but scroll by scroll" (56). Indeed, the biblical manuscripts and commentaries found among the Dead Sea Scrolls show that they were copied and explained "scroll by scroll."

Similarly the Letter of Aristeas (177) speaks of the Pentateuch as made up of a number of scrolls, each protected by its own cover and kept together in a vessel.

b. In accord with the distinction between "the Law" (Gen–Deut) and the rest of the Hebrew Bible, "the Prophets" and "the Writings," a twofold differentiation emerged in interpretive activity: Halaka and Haggada, or, Ethics and Theology. "The Law," and the Halaka based on it, refer to the committal to written form of the manifestations of the divine will for Israel's action and behavior, while "the Prophets" and "the Writings" confirm, guard, and unfold the ethical teaching through story, parable, proverb, prayer, and song. While "the Law" and its Halaka increasingly functioned as the constitution of Israel both in the Land of Canaan and in the Dispersion, the traditions of "the Prophets" and of "the Writings," as well as narrative portions of the Pentateuch, invited free narrative re-creation of its motifs, themes, and patterns. Thus the legal portions of the first five sections of the Hebrew Bible, together with their interpretations for successive periods, prescribe the ethics for Israel in the form of halakic midrash, notably in Mishnah and Talmud, but the stories of the Pentateuch and of "the Prophets and the Writings" evoke theological reflection and engender storytelling of great variety in the form of haggadic midrash. Three important features of haggadic midrash call for comment.

(1) While the procedures of halakic midrash are minutely prescribed and carefully guarded, the narrative re-creation of non-legal biblical texts is a free and open-ended activity, spurring the imagination of both the haggadists and their audiences. Thus it creates a great variety of interpretations, many of which are preserved in commentary form. Two anthologies are notable: in English there is Louis Ginzberg's bringing together and retelling, in canonical sequence, *The Legends of the Jews,* 7 vols. (1909–68), while in Hebrew *The Book of Haggada,* edited by Bialik and Revnizki (5th printing; 1973) is similarly arranged.

(2) Relative freedom from exegetical rules is a characteristic feature of haggadic midrash. Thus Kadushin emphasizes that

"in haggadic interpretation the Biblical texts serve as spring-board merely, as a stimulus, whereas halakic interpretation of Scripture employs systematically ordered procedures set forth in hermeneutic rules" (126). Because haggadic activity is not restricted and regulated as halakic interpretation, "the haggadic method required only that there be a connection between a Biblical text and a haggadic idea" (120). In fact, "*any kind* of sequence" (122, my italics) suffices to establish the desired connection. Unlike the verse-by-verse commentaries found for instance among the Dead Sea Scrolls, free midrash is made up of narratives and visions that are spun from a few dates and names in Scripture, and connected with it only by "a thin thread" (Betz, 79–80).

(3) It is a matter of definition to what extent and in what manner the non-legal portions of Scripture are themselves already the creation of haggadic activity. The post-exilic work of the Chronicler(s) may be defined as a midrash on 1 Sam 31–2 Kgs 25/Hag–Mal. It demonstrates great interpretive freedom in that it (*a*) ignores (or skips over) large sections of its "text," for instance all passages in Sam and Kgs that deal with the Kingdom of Israel; (*b*) considerably expands those of its biblical base texts that deal with King David as Temple builder and the Davidic dynasty as Temple patron; and (*c*) adds new stories wherever that serves its purpose. Through deletions, expansions, and additions the Chronicler(s)' work heightens or more sharply contrasts with each other features of its "scripture." Moreover, it spiritualizes some and nationalizes others. Ecles is another example of a haggadic midrash within the Hebrew Bible in that it quotes and critically weighs inherited wisdom themes.

Accordingly, Seeligmann's study of the presuppositions of midrashic exegesis argues that its beginnings reach back into the formative stages of the Hebrew Scriptures and that the antecedents of haggadic activity are found in the writings of the New Testament and other early Christian literature, the Apocrypha and Pseudepigrapha of both Testaments, the Dead Sea

Scrolls, the Septuagint, as well as in the passages of the Hebrew Bible itself where older biblical texts are cited or to which they allude (151). It is noteworthy in the context of this study that Seeligmann includes the writings of the New Testament in this list.

   c. Seeligmann presents several examples that show how a biblical motif remains alive within the changes that it undergoes in later biblical writing and in post-biblical haggadic activity. Thus he explores (155–157) the motif "wealth gained through injustice or violence will eventually benefit not the evil person who accumulated it, but a righteous and brave man" (Prov 13:22, 28:8, Job 27:16–17). Ecles inverts and theologizes the motif by having God assign to the sinner the task of gathering and heaping up "only to give to one who pleases God" (Ecles 2:26). Sirach, in turn, inverts and psychologizes the motif as Ecles had presented it: He exhorts the well-to-do man not to be stingy to himself, for "whoever accumulates by depriving himself, accumulates for others" (Sir 14:3–4). Seeligmann notes that Ecles, even though it inverted the scriptural motif, was careful to retain two of its characteristic formulations as connector words or phrases, that is, "one who is good before God" and "the sinner" (Prov 13:22/Ecles 2:26).

   The example demonstrates that the biblical tradition is "in perpetual motion," that canonization does not terminate that movement, and that a biblical text is capable of a variety of interpretations (Seeligmann, 153). Kadushin sees in the emergence of many and different interpretations in relation to one and the same text that feature which distinguishes haggadic activity from scientific or philosophical interpretations (104–107; similarly Seeligmann, 160). Fiebig observes in the same vein that the various versions of the same parable in the synoptic gospels are examples of "re-creative art" (1925, 115). Thus haggadic activity is foremost not a literary product but "an attitude to Scripture" (Patte, 117), which in the first place does not interpret a clearly defined and literarily fixed text by another one but which sustains a still fluid, not yet congealed one

by circling it playfully (Seeligmann, 150). The headings of the
two main sections of Heinemann's full discussion of *The Ways
of Haggada,* that is, "Creative Historiography" and "Creative
Philology" (15–95, 96–164), appropriately highlight the inge-
nuity and inventiveness of the haggadists. After all, they are
persuaded that what Scripture tells about a person or event "is
but a small fraction of what might have been told" (Ginzberg
IV, 86, comp. VI 250).

   d. The classification of haggadic procedures proposed by
Heinemann is based on two considerations. On the one hand,
there is the conviction that each part of Scripture, even its individual letters, are important as they stand and in their own
right, quite apart from their narrower and wider contexts. On
the other hand, haggadic creativity takes seriously the persua-
sion that Scripture was not written to entertain or to shock, but
to instruct, that is, to create also new compositions in order to
carry out that mandate. Thus haggadists may base a midrash
(1) on a single letter, (2) on a single word, (3) on a phrase, or
(4) on a text section. But they may also (5) create an altogether new composition. A discussion of each in relation to Mk
is indicated.

   (1) Heinemann shows how haggadists generate a midrash on
the basis of a single letter of the alphabet. One of his examples
is illustrated by reference to the second gospel (97). He observes
that the midrashists can convert the (Hebrew) dative case, using the letter "l" to signify what is classified by grammarians as
the dative of emphasis, into a dative of possession, which can
be expressed in the same manner, that is, through the prefixing
of "l" (with the same vocalization in the Masoretic Text). Thus
the dative case in Ex 12:1, "This month shall be for you...," is
interpreted by some haggadists as expressing the notion of blessing on those to whom it is addressed, that is, as a possession to
be celebrated and enjoyed. Heinemann then refers in a footnote
to Mk 2:27 as another example of such interpretive transformation of the dative of emphasis: Mark's Jesus argues that taking
ears of grain on a sabbath to still one's hunger is permitted,

because "the sabbath was instituted for the sake of man, and not man for the sake of the sabbath" (Mk 2:27). This claim is derived from Lev 16:31 ("The sabbath shall be for you...."; comp. Lev 23:32) in the same manner as the example of Ex 12:1 discussed above. Further examples of haggadic activity based on a single letter are found in Heinemann, 103–107.

(2) In relation to the midrashic use of a single word or of a name found in a biblical text he notes that haggadists usually ignore — and at times even contradict — the syntactic and thematic contexts. Crucial is only that the same word or name appear in both scriptural base text and midrash. As connectors they establish the warrant for the interpretive creativity. Modern interpreters, to be sure, consider such isolation of a word from its contexts an arbitrary procedure, but ancient audiences, steeped in biblical imagery, evidently were willing to build reflection and writing on such correspondences. Heinemann's examples illustrate how this hermeneutic activity moves from the scriptural use of a word or name to its employment in midrash; one example (114–115) is a midrash on "almsgiving" ($ṣdqh$) which is based on biblical texts relating to "mutual loyalty" ($ṣdqh$). Similarly the second gospel establishes correlations between its text units and their intended scriptural referents.

Given Mk's hermeneutic of concealment and disclosure (see 7.1.2 above), the evangelist's employment of a variety of connector words, names, numbers, and phrases has a cumulative effect. Thus the recognition of the relationship between the gospel and its scriptural antecedent to which the audience is at first tentatively drawn is increasingly reinforced and finally secured in the awareness of the presence of a scriptural paradigm in the entire gospel. For example, by introducing notable words such as "good news," "hundredfold," or "camel and wealth," each an important notion in its immediate context, the evangelist keeps evoking 1 Kgs 17–2 Kgs 13. On the other hand, the direct equation of John with Elijah (Mk 9:11–13; comp. 1:2–11, esp. 1:8, and 6:14–29) is more openly evidence of this haggadic procedure. Analogies are the haggadic equations of Rome with

Esau (Heinemann, 32–34) and of the Greeks with the Chaldeans (1QpHab II 10–15).

(3) The midrashists' use of phrases and sentences (Heinemann, 131–136) is similar to that of words and names in that also here biblical contexts are often ignored. Heinemann concludes his discussion with the question of how far the setting aside of the context eliminates altogether the literal meaning of the text for the sake of supplying biblical warrants for the midrash proffered. One may consider in the light of his conclusions the evangelist's use of connector phrases, such as the exclamation "you have come … to destroy," uttered by the man obsessed by an unclean spirit who was present in the synagogue at Capernaum when Jesus began his preaching there (Mk 1:24; comp. 1 Kgs 17:18b; see 5.1.5 above), and two of the prohibitions with which the twelve disciples are sent out, directing them to take "no money … nor two cloaks" (Mk 6:8–9; comp. 2 Kgs 5:22b and 6.2.3 above).

(4) Heinemann demonstrates how haggadic activity related to shorter or longer sections of biblical text produced a variety of midrashic compositions (137–161), some of which may be characterized outright as "new teaching" (Mk 1:27; comp. Heinemann, 138–140). This type of interpretive activity, more encompassing than the examples discussed in the preceding paragraphs, readily led to allegorization, such as the interpretation of Songs of Solomon as portrayal of divine love for Israel, or to the creation of (new) historical references or of (additional) ethical demands (137). Heinemann observes that both early Judaism and early Christianity engaged in this kind of haggadic creativity, then points out that the former tended to locate its equations within the constraints of the observance of "the Law," while early Christian haggadists tended to emphasize the universality of the biblical perspective (149–150). At any rate, several of the motifs in Mk's narrative execution (see chapter 5 above) are analogies to the hermeneutic activity discussed by Heinemann, for instance, the story of the call of the first four disciples as carriers of "the good news" that draws its plot from the

narrative of the crucial role that the four lepers play in encountering and making known the good news of Samaria's delivery from the Aramean siege (2 Kgs 7:9, 3–8; see 5.2.2 above) or the evangelist's use of the martyrdom paradigm of the Naboth story in the narration of Jesus' passion and death (1 Kgs 21:1–29; see 6.2.3 above).

e. Midrashists also create altogether new compositions by telling stories that are similar to those narrated in Scripture. They may transform the plot by heightening or lessening, by duplicating or graduating, by inverting, paralleling, or equating. The following examples illustrate several of these haggadic transformations.

(1) Heightening of a biblical motif appears in a story about Israel's crossing the Jordan into the land of promise:

> Scarcely had the priests, who at this solemn moment took the place of the Levites as bearers of the Ark, set foot in the Jordan, when the waters of the river were piled up to a height of three hundred miles. All the peoples of the earth were witnesses of the wonder. [Ginzberg IV, 5]

Another haggadic narrative heightens by way of contrast:

> When on Mount Carmel Elijah had handed to the Baal prophets their heifer the priests sought to deceive the people. They undermined the altar, and Hiel hid himself under it with the purpose of igniting a fire at the mention of the word Baal. But God sent a serpent to kill him. [Ginzberg IV, 198]

A similar heightening is found in both stories of the miraculous feeding in Mk (6:32–44, 8:1–9): In comparison to its scriptural model, Elisha's feeding of a hundred persons with twenty barley loaves and some garden produce, all numerical values are made higher or lower in order to portray the miracle as a greater one in quantitative terms. Thus, to the hundred persons fed by the prophet correspond 5,000 fed by Jesus, to the twenty loaves and the produce available to Elisha correspond only five loaves and two fishes that are at Jesus' disposal, to the one servant through whom the prophet serves the people correspond in the Jesus narrative twelve disciples, and with the notation in the Elisha story that food was "left over" correlates the observation in Mk that twelve baskets were filled with what was "left over."

(2) An example of the doubling of a biblical motif is found in a haggadic midrash told about Joshua before Jericho. The mother of the enemy king Shobac raised by magic seven walls around the city in order to counter more effectively Joshua's seven marches around the city, but still could not save it from Joshua (Ginzberg IV, 15). A similar procedure is the evangelist's doubling of the miraculous feeding (Mk 6:32–44/8:1–9; see 4.3.1 above for the compositional effect in Mk) in comparison to only one scriptural base story in 1 Kgs 17–2 Kgs 13. By the same token, an example of tripling is found in Jesus' condemnation of the offending hand, foot, and eye (Mk 9:42–48), creating a serialization (see 4.3.2 above). This feature is discussed by Kadushin:

> We may have several consecutive interpretations of the same Biblical verse, each of them an independent entity.... But even when passages are connected in exegetical Haggadah, they are connected by a device, used also in midrashic works of other types.... A statement interpreting a Biblical text may be followed by other statements, each joined to the one preceding by an association of ideas, whilst none but the first is an interpretation of the Biblical verse which is the homiletic origin for the entire passage. [61]

Thus it is not unusual in haggadic midrash to tell more than one story in relation to one biblical base text. Kadushin observes that "often placed side by side are many different interpretations of the same verse or the same event.... This is amply illustrated by almost any midrashic text we happen to choose...." The first midrash introduces others on the same theme, which are simply

identified as "another matter," that is, further possible interpretation (71–72). These serializations may even bring together
different value concepts held by haggadists (73–74). Thus the
cluster of controversy stories in Mk 2:1–3:6 (see 6.2.1, also 4.3.2
above) covers debated issues also discussed by Mark's Jesus, and
does so by way of preview of the gospel in its entirety.

(3) Heinemann also shows (49–58) that haggadic activity
was eager to discern graduations in the behavior of biblical figures or events. He observes that educational considerations at
times avoid either/or schematizations in order to mirror the
graduations found in human life and attitudes (54). Such graduations may appear in formulations of parables. For instance,
in a midrash on Est the advance of evil in the world is compared
to a king entering his vineyard and finding himself confronted
successively by three kinds of foes: the first begins to pick the
gleanings reserved for the poor, the second cuts off grape clus-
ters, and the third sets out to tear up the vines themselves. The
three are equated with Pharaoh, Nebuchadnezzar, and Haman
(54). This staggering is reminiscent of Mk's parable of the sower
(Mk 4:3–20), where the seed that has fallen on good soil bears
fruit in a graduated fashion.

Heinemann observes that post-biblical sages "characterized
like Hellenistic writers, only more so, degrees among the righteous and the sinners, . . . and introduced intermediary stages
among the completely righteous and the totally sinful" (54).
He also discusses the use of comparisons that employ analogies
based on scriptural antecedents (61). One example he quotes
differentiates reactions to affliction that human beings may be
called upon to endure:

> There are four who were afflicted. Job was afflicted and
> fought back. Abraham was afflicted and laughed in re-
> sponse. Hezekiah was afflicted and implored the One who
> loved him for mercy. David said, "On what does the afflic-
> tion depend? Make yourself firm in the Name." [Midrash
> on Psalms 26, 2; Heinemann, 61]

Here four kinds of scriptural responses to suffering are identified, counted, grouped, and differentiated in terms of the human response to the affliction. Thus a graduation is surfaced. Job was least respectful of God, David most so. Here a didactic concern seems to be at work, because audiences may gauge themselves in terms of the perfection of their own obedience and observance.

(4) Motif inversion as haggadic principle may be found in instances where the biblical base text is perceived to be embarrassing. Thus the Aramaic Bible paraphrases (Targumim) seek to overcome the offense perceived in relation to Num 12:1, according to which Moses had married a Cushite woman, that is, a non-Israelite. The paraphrases claim that he had in fact married a beautiful woman or that she was not a Cushite at all (Patte, 64). Another midrash inverts the statement of Dt 26:5 in a similar manner. While the biblical reading speaks of Jacob as "a perishing Aramean," the midrash reads: "An Aramean [presumably Laban] sought to let my father perish...." Thus it was not Israel's progenitor who was close to death but his uncle Laban who indeed is said to have taken advantage of Jacob more than once (Silberman, 324–325).

A possible example of inversion in Mk's work is the brief story of Jesus' response to children brought to him so that he bless them (Mk 10:13–16). Jesus' reaction is, by way of contrast, reminiscent of the brief story of Elisha's cursing of children who had mocked him when he left the city of Jericho (2 Kgs 2:23–24). Thus the gospel contrasts Jesus and Elisha, while in other texts it shows him exceeding the man from Abel-meholah. It is noteworthy that unease with Elisha's cursing generated a midrash preserved in the *Babylonian Talmud* (Sota 46b):

> R. Jochanan said in the name of R. Meir: Whoever does not escort others or allow himself to be escorted is as though he sheds blood; for had the men of Jericho escorted Elisha he would not have stirred up bears against the children....

f. Heightening, doubling, graduation, and inversion of biblical motifs and plots may take the haggadist far from the scriptural base. This is even more the case when a midrash is formulated in which a correspondence in numerical terms is the structuring principle of composition.

References to numbers found within a biblical text may be used in order to relate a midrash to it. Thus a story on the spy episode (Num 13–14) speaks of the explorers' forty-day journey through Canaan and claims that the duration of their mission corresponds to the forty years of Israel's wandering in the desert toward Canaan (Heinemann, 65–66). Also the second gospel lets Jesus' sojourn in the wilderness, immediately after his baptism (Mk 1:12–13; comp. 1:9–11), last forty days, echoing Elijah's forty days' and forty nights' journey to the Horeb (1 Kgs 19:1–10).

(1) Apart from the two further numerical correlations already discussed (see 5.2.2 and 5.2.3 above), there are more examples. Thus the appointment of twelve apostles (Mk 3:13–19) reflects the all-Israel orientation of the Elijah/Elisha Narrative, which tells that the man from Tishbe restored the deserted altar on Mount Carmel with twelve stones, each representing one of the twelve tribes of Israel (1 Kgs 18:32; comp. 19:19). By the same token, the seven baskets of leftovers from Jesus' second miraculous feeding (Mk 8:1–9) may evoke in the audience the numerical element in the reference to Israel's remnant of 7,000 who have not allowed themselves to be enticed into apostasy (1 Kgs 19:18). A telling numerical correspondence in Mk's parable of the sower (Mk 4:3–20) is the numerical value "hundredfold": Those who respond most fully to the divine summons conveyed through Jesus' mission "bear fruit" a hundredfold. This number corresponds to the action of Obadiah, King Ahab's God-fearing chief steward, who "bore fruit" by rescuing a hundred prophets from Queen Jezebel's slaughter of the LORD's prophets (1 Kgs 18:4, 13).

(2) Easily the most striking numerical correspondence between the second gospel and the Elijah/Elisha Narrative is the counting of Jesus' deeds of power as discussed in 2.1 and 2.6

above. With his healing of the deaf-mute person (Mk 7:31–37) the man from Nazareth has satisfied the standard set by Elisha in that he has performed sixteen miracles. The miracles that Jesus then proceeds to do (found in Mk 8–16) show that he exceeds Elisha by as many powerful deeds as Elisha exceeded Elijah. Such enumeration of the prophet's miracles is already attested in the Elisha Story (2 Kgs 8:1–6); small wonder that post-biblical haggadists elaborated the numerical motif further in the way in which the second gospel attests it. Ginzberg's narrative summary of midrashic storytelling in relation to Elisha, already noted in 2.6, shows that Mk was not the only one who counted Elisha's deeds of power and elaborated the motif:

> Elijah's promise to bestow a double portion of his wondrous spirit upon his disciples was realized instantaneously. During his life Elisha performed sixteen miracles, and eight was all his master had performed. [IV, 239]

To be sure, Ginzberg also observes that "neither the eight miracles of Elijah nor the sixteen of Elisha are enumerated in the Midrashim extant today"; he adds that a phrase used in this context in the Great Midrash on Genesis and Exodus "undoubtedly refers to an old source where they were given in detail" (VI, 343–344). In other words, haggadic creativity not only counted miracles, but also claimed that Elisha's miracles exceeded by eight those of Elijah, and that in keeping with the conveyance of a double portion of Elijah's spirit on the prophet. Thus the second gospel employs the same interpretive procedure and expands on it in order to generate one of its basic compositional-structural features: Jesus exceeds Elisha by as many miracles as Elisha exceeded Elijah.

g. The correspondence between haggadic midrash and its scriptural base may be the identification of biblical figures or objects either with those of other biblical texts or with those of the midrashist's own day. Thus Melchizedeq may be equated with Shem, or Balaam with Laban, or Jacob's daughter Dina with Job's wife (Patte, 69). By the same token, Elijah may be equated with Phinehas and/or John the Baptist (Heinemann, 30), Esau with Rome (Heinemann, 32–34), or the Chaldeans of the Hebrew Bible with the Greeks of a later period (1QpHab II 10–15). Similarly, biblical objects may be equated with those of the haggadist's place and time. Thus in the Damascus Document (CD VIII 14–21) a series of five equations of items mentioned in Am 5:26–27 is given: (1) The book of the Law = the heart of the king; (2) the king = the congregation; (3) the basis of the statutes = the book of the Prophets; (4) the star = the interpreter of the Law; (5) the staff = the prince of the whole congregation. These correspondences are of the same nature as those explicitly made in Jesus' solution of the parable of the sower (Mk 4:14–20) and as those apparently implied in the evangelist's narration of the martyrdom of John the Baptist (Mk 6:21–29): King Herod and Queen Herodias correspond to King Ahab and his queen respectively, while John's fate is that with which Elijah had been threatened by Jezebel (comp. 1 Kgs 19:1–3).

Since these interpretive equations primarily reflect correspondences perceived in terms of attitudes and actions, consistency in the correlation of a biblical figure with one and the same person in the haggadist's time and place is not necessarily maintained. Thus a scriptural personage may be identified with more than one person. Betz points out (79) that 1QpHab equates "the righteous one" of Hab 1:4 with "the Teacher of Righteousness" (1QpHab I 13), while "the righteous one" of Hab 2:4 is equated in the same writing with "the doers of the law," that is, with the whole congregation (1QpHab VIII 1–3). Similarly the second gospel identifies Jesus at first with Elijah (comp. Mk 1:12–13 with 1 Kgs 19:1–10), more usually with Elisha (comp. Mk 1:14–7:37 with 2 Kgs 2:13–8:6; see 2.1–2.5 above), at times with Jehu (comp. Mk 14:3–9 with 2 Kgs 9:1–10), but also with Naboth (comp. Mk 14:1–15:37 [especially 12:6–8] with 1 Kgs 21:1–29; see 6.2.3 above). For haggadists the conceptualization of the events of their times as re-enactments of basic biblical plots was the overriding concern (see Baeck's observations dis-

cussed in 7.1.1 above), to which consistency in the identification
of actors in the plots had to be subordinated.

h. Finally, the haggadists are freely creative when they reflect on aspects or elements of the biblical heritage and make
these the medium of new (or re-)conceptualizations. Thus al-
legories can be formulated in order to set forth philosophies of
history, or biblical texts used as springboards for the elaboration of religious psychologies of individuals or groups, or miracle stories told as affirmation of the divine presence also in the
midrashist's time; see Fiebig 1911 and 1912 for a collection of
representative samples. A review of some of these in relation to
Mk's hermeneutic activity is instructive.

(1) On the one hand, midrashists draw on a variety of motifs from flora, fauna, agriculture, architecture, trade, and public
life. For instance, tree imagery is favored in the Hebrew Bible as
well as in post-biblical parabling. Thus Ezek 17:1–24 portrays
through the parable-allegory of the cedar on Mount Lebanon
and the twig that becomes a vine a part of the history of God's
people as the parabler perceives it. Or, according to the Genesis Apocryphon (XIX), Abraham foresees in a dream Sarah's
and his own future in Egypt. As such it is a parable-allegory
based on Gen 12–13, in which the patriarch corresponds to a
cedar tree that men seek to cut down, while the matriarch is
equated with a palm tree that they will allow to remain stand-
ing. Abraham describes the dream to his wife and she agrees
to say to the Egyptians that Abraham is her brother. Thus the
dream justifies what in fact is, at least in its immediate literary
context, a misrepresentation.

The second gospel employs tree imagery several times: There
is the parable of the mustard tree's phenomenal growth (Mk
4:30–32), the parable of the withered fig tree (Mk 11:12–14,
20–21), and that of the fig tree whose sprouting leaves indicate
the approach of summer (Mk 13:28–29). Similarly, the motif
of a field and of the growth of seeds sown on it is employed
by the second evangelist (Mk 4:3–20, 4:26–29) as well as by
a seer-theologian who composed a work toward the end of the

first century C.E. (4 Ez 8:41–45). The theme of a vineyard as
interpretive category in relation to Israel is employed by the
second evangelist in the parable of the faithless stewards (Mk
12:1–12) as well as by haggadists who compare the LORD to
a vineyard owner: On entering his planting God finds himself
joined by three progressively more destructive figures: Pharaoh,
Nebuchadnezzar, and Haman (Heinemann, 54). The vineyard
imagery seems directly suggested to Mk by the story of Naboth's
vineyard (1 Kgs 21:1–29) — a composition parabolic in a manner
similar to Isaiah's vineyard song (Is 5:1–7).

(2) On the other hand, spiritualizations of biblical texts may
explore the psychology of the God-fearing individual. Thus the
four modes of divine revelation mentioned in 1 Kgs 19:11–14, the
first three of which are found by Elijah not to mediate revelation,
are an example of such hermeneutic activity. The four means of
disclosure in fact refer to stages in life:

> The four phenomena that God sent before His appear-
> ance — wind, earthquake, fire and a still small voice —
> were to instruct Elijah about the destiny of man. God told
> Elijah that these four represent the worlds through which
> man must pass: the first stands for this world, fleeting as
> the wind; the earthquake is the day of death, which makes
> the human body to tremble and quake; fire is the tribunal
> in Gehenna, and the still small voice is the Last Judgment,
> when there will be none than God alone. [Ginzberg IV,
> 200]

Mark's narration of the two stories of Jesus' granting sight (and
spiritual insight) to a man from Bethsaida and later to the beg-
gar near Jericho (Mk 8:22–26, 10:46–52) are comparable. The
first story illustrates how the internal illumination takes place
in stages while the other portrays an immediate eye opening.
Thus the two stories point to two ways in which persons may
respond to Jesus; in this respect they are comparable to a similar compositional staging of the two feeding narratives (see 2.6
above).

i. Haggadic miracle stories serve to attest the presence of divine power in the same way in which their biblical counterparts affirm it for their settings. Fiebig's collection (1911) presents and discusses miracle stories from Tannaitic and Amoraic periods (before/after approx. 200 C.E.). Some of the Tannaitic examples parallel Markan texts: Healing by prayer (Fiebig 1911, 19–22/Mk 9:14–29), multiplication of bread (Fiebig 1911, 22–24/Mk 6:32–44, 8:1–9), control of dangerous demons (Fiebig 1911, 25–26/Mk 1:23–28, 5:1–20, 7:24–30), uprooting a tree (Fiebig 1911, 32–33/Mk 11:12–14, 20–21), stilling of a sea (Fiebig 1911, 33/Mk 4:35–41, 6:45–51), healing through the name of a master teacher (Fiebig 1911, 35–36/Mk 3:15, 6:7, 12–13, 16–17), and even revival of a dead person (Fiebig 1911, 36–38/Mk 5:21–24, 35–43). The second gospel thus affirms in its way what these haggadic stories attest in their ways: The certainty of divine intervention here and now, and that in accord with the patterns of the Scriptures.

j. By way of summary of this representative, though not exhaustive, review of the ways of haggadic midrash it may be said that the haggadists did not set their own time over against that of the Bible. The two were for them, as Patte puts it, "a synthetic unity," because the "different periods are closely interrelated." Due to this appropriation of the past and of its legacy, Patte continues,

> the meaning of an event is to be understood together with similar events which occurred before and after it. We could express this by saying that such an event is pre-figured (or prophesied) by an event of the past and pre-figures (or prophesies) events of the future. Yet this is not exactly so. Rather ... there is an implicit unity, or better a basic identity between these events. [69]

While Patte speaks here specifically of the hermeneutic of Aramaic paraphrase-translations, what he says is applicable to midrashic activity generally. Heinemann puts it this way: "The future is enacted in the past" (34), or "One must view what happens to the fathers as a sign of what the future holds for the sons" (Heinemann, 33, comp. Seeligmann, 175).

8.2   Roman-Hellenistic Imitation

The review of theory and practice of haggadic midrash and its relation to Mk has shown that several of the gospel's unique features relating to 1 Kgs 17–2 Kgs 13 are paralleled in the works that the hermeneutic activity of early Judaism created. On the other hand, there remain at least two of its features, the concealment of the assumed paradigm and the intermingling of biblical, even extra-biblical traditions, that are not clearly paralleled in haggadic compositions. Hence the question: Do other Roman- or Jewish-Hellenistic literary creations, especially those clearly composed according to the rhetorical principle of imitation ("imitatio"), throw light on the gospel? More specifically, has this issue been pursued with reference to the gospels? Two recent publications do so: Thomas Louis Brodie's essay "Greco-Roman Imitation of Texts as Partial Guide to Luke's Use of Sources" (1983a) explores the question with relation to Lk/Acts, supported by further articles (1983b; 1983c) that demonstrate in detailed analysis the approach advocated in the programmatic essay. On the other hand, George A. Kennedy's *New Testament Interpretation Through Rhetorical Criticism* (1984) illustrates how sections of the New Testament, including three contained in the first, third, and fourth gospels, may be analyzed as examples of two ancient categories of rhetorical activity. Since these publications are readily accessible in English, their discussion in relation to this study can limit itself to the search for analogies to the hermeneutic activity found in the second gospel.

   a. The title of Brodie's dissertation (1981) summarizes his thesis: Lk/Acts is "a systematic rewriting and updating of the Elijah-Elisha Narrative in 1 and 2 Kings." Thus his analysis identifies for Lk/Acts the same scriptural model that I identify for Mk. Brodie's and my conclusions, reached independently, not only reinforce each other in terms of the method of analysis adopted and their results, but also support the assumption that "the synoptic gospel" type is due to the basic structuring function of 1 Kgs 17–2 Kgs 13 within Mk, Mt, and Lk/Acts (comp. 7.1.5 above). By the same token, Brodie also emphasizes that it is appropriate to speak of imitation merely as a partial guide to the evangelist's use of sources, and thus points to the probable presence of additional compositional patterns and motifs. His thorough and cautious argumentation is persuasive and thus raises the question whether his identification of the nature of Lk's relation to 1 Kgs 17–2 Kgs 13 is applicable also to Mk. In other words, is imitation a partial guide to the composition and narrative execution of the second gospel?

(1) A brief review of Brodie's programmatic discussion of theory and practice of imitation is in order. He notes that "no single clear-cut theory of literary imitation" existed in antiquity (1983a, 19), rather, it was "a multi-faceted concept" comprising "different activities" (1983a, 20). One of these is "inventive imitation," which Brodie describes as

> a tense blend of *imitatio* and *inventio* (creativity), a com-
> bining of old material with new. Thus, while Quintilian
> took it for granted that a large part of art consists of im-
> itation, ... he also realized that sheer imitation is not suf-
> ficient ... and pointed out that every art involves *inventio*
> not only at its inception but also throughout its continuing
> existence. ... Much of what Greco-Roman writers have to
> say about imitation is concerned precisely with this rather
> unpredictable blending of fidelity and creativity. [1983a,
> 20]

He concludes his survey of the theory of literary imitation with the observation that

> imitation is not a narrow category of literary dependence.
> It is, rather, a whole world of transformation, the broad
> context within which diverse writers combine tradition and
> innovation. It is not tidy and predictable. On the contrary,

since it is a complex arena of artistry, it allows for constant surprises. [1983a, 22]

Thus free interplay between literary legacy and hermeneutic activity characterizes Greco-Roman *imitatio* as much as Jewish-Hellenistic haggadic midrash. Neither is, in Brodie's words, "tidy and predictable" and both are a blend of faithfulness to tradition with creative interpretation, allowing "for constant surprises." The words of Matthew's Jesus at the end of the parable chapter (Mt 13:1–52) illustrate the point: "...every scribe who has been trained for the kingdom of heaven is like a householder who brings out of his treasure what is new and what is old."

(2) A discussion of the results of one of Brodie's papers (1983b) is instructive. In "The Accusing and Stoning of Naboth (1 Kgs 21:8–13) as One Component of the Stephen Text (Acts 6:9–14; 7:58a)" he presents the case for this thesis. Before he shows the correspondence in plot and narration and deals with possible objections (1983b, 420–431, note especially the synopsis of the two texts and the summary), he briefly indicates that Luke casts Stephen's martyrdom in a manner that "there are at least four points of similarity" with that of Jesus as told in the third gospel: "Being led into the sanhedrin by the concerted leadership of the people (Acts 6:12; cf. Lk 22:66); the accusation concerning the temple (Acts 6:14a; cf. Mk 14:57–58); the visitation of the Son of Man (Acts 7:55, 56; cf. Lk 22:69; Mk 14:62); and the last words (Acts 7:59–60; cf. Lk 23:34, 46)" (1983b, 419). Brodie thus shows that for Luke the Naboth story supplied the basic conceptual model for Jesus' martyrdom. This is the very conclusion reached in this study in relation to the second evangelist (see 6.2.3 above).

In this context Brodie also discusses the adequacy of the term "midrash" as description of Luke's hermeneutic activity and, adopting a narrower definition of the term, comes to the conclusion that "it seems better to avoid" it (1983b, 430). It is Luke's concealment of the scriptural model — one of the four unique features also of Mk — which, as "use of unacknowledged sources seems to belong not so much to the techniques of midrash, but to those of Greco-Roman paraphrase and imitation." Brodie's formulation seems to indicate that a fully descriptive category has not yet been found.

b. New Testament Interpretation Through Rhetorical Criticism by George A. Kennedy (1984) explores, after an introductory description of rhetorical criticism, examples of "deliberative rhetoric" in Mt's Sermon on the Mount (Mt 5–7; Kennedy, 39–63) and in Lk's Sermon on the Plain (Lk 6; Kennedy, 63–67), as well as Jn 13–17 as example of "epideictic rhetoric." "The Rhetoric of the Gospels" is analyzed in a separate chapter (Kennedy, 97–113); its three pages devoted to Mk call for comment. Kennedy does not subject the gospel as a literary unit to the method of inquiry he employs in the chapters on sections of Mt, Lk, and Jn; thus he does not address the issue pursued in this study. On the other hand, he categorizes Mk "as an example of what may be called radical Christian rhetoric, a form of 'sacred language' characterized by assertion and absolute claims of authoritative truth without evidence or logical argument" and briefly elaborates on this observation (104–105).

His characterization of Mk raises the question of the constraint that makes the second gospel a form of "radical Christian rhetoric." The thesis advanced in this study may supply the answer: The evangelist assumes that the disciples are initiated into the secret of the Kingdom and therefore know its scenario (Mk 4:10–12; see 2.4 above); thus the gospel can narrate its progress as re-enactment of the already established plot. Kennedy's further observation that it is more likely that the first gospel moderated and transformed Mk rather than the reverse also supports the conclusion reached in this study (see 7.2 above):

That Matthew might have recast Mark's account into a more rationalizing rhetoric is a better possibility. If so, he was seeking to adapt the gospel to an audience which in

this, as in other respects, thought in different ways or had
different needs. For any among his readers familiar with
Mark, the preservation of some similarities of expression
would have been reassuring and have helped to authenticate his work. [107]

In short, while Kennedy's observations on Mk provide a supportive framework for the analysis presented in this study, they
do not directly relate to its findings.

8.3   In Search of Descriptive Categories

Evidently more discussion is needed before the two hermeneutical activities of haggadic midrash and rhetorical imitation can
be satisfactorily defined in relation to each other and, if applicable, to the hermeneutical activities that Brodie and I discern
as those of the evangelists. By the same token, narratological
insights that employ neither category — or do so in a tentative
manner — must be considered.

For instance, Lou H. Silberman suggested in a private com-
munication (Dec. 17, 1985) "that the 'plot' of the Elijah-Elisha
stories may have been taken over by the author of Mark, and he
then distributed the events of Jesus' career, what [the Russian
literary critic Viktor] Shklovskij calls *fabula*, along that con-
tinuum." Rather than identifying this compositional-narrative
procedure as midrash, Silberman suggests describing it as "patterned storytelling." This manner of categorizing Mk's hermeneutical activity has the advantage of working with an interpretive framework that is not as defined as those of haggadic
midrash and of rhetorical imitation. On the other hand, given
the elasticity of either as recognized already by their ancient
practitioners, patterned storytelling may well be located at some
intersection of the two, illustrating the intermingling of patterns
to which Robbins as well as Brodie (1983b, 430–431) refer.

Chapter 9

Conclusion

9.1 The Audience of the Gospel

Who were the addressees of a work that is full of clues and allusions and that assumes that its readers can and will recognize with growing clarity the outline and details of its literary-conceptual model once they permit the initial identification of John the Baptist with Elijah of Tishbe to engage their interest and to trigger search and reflection? Is it reasonable to posit the existence of an audience steeped in their Bible to such an extent that the discovered correspondences to 1 Kgs 17–2 Kgs 13 may be expected to make the evangelist's case?

a. If the thesis here advanced is granted, such a community of readers must have existed — audiences to whom, by the same token, the other gospels also seem to be addressed. Apart from the possibility that the other evangelists were the partners in the conversation (a question that cannot be pursued in this study), figures appearing in Mk as interested in — or supportive of — Jesus' mission, are candidates. Especially Joseph of Arimathea (15:42–47) and the Scripture scholar enquiring concerning the first commandment (12:28–34a) are to be noted because they are expressly related to "the Kingdom of God": the latter is found by Jesus not to "be far from" it while the former is characterized as one who is "also himself looking for the Kingdom of God."

b. Such anticipation assumes an expectation model not unlike the one proposed by 4 Ezr, another writer of the first century
C.E.: After the LORD has shown to the seer "a multitude of the
signs" that he will do in the last times without, however, indicating when they will appear, the seer is told, "When you see
that a certain part of the predicted signs are past, then you will
know that it is the very time when the Most High is about to
visit the world... " (4 Ezr 8:63–9:2). Thus Joseph of Arimathea
is portrayed not only as preserving Jesus' body in a rock-hewn
cave as his counterpart Obadiah, the God-fearing chief steward
of King Ahab, had done (see 6.1.6), but also as a type of the
readers of the gospel: versed in his people's traditions as well as
living in expectation of the manifestation of God's Kingdom.

c. Put more broadly, the gospel's audience constitutes itself to the extent to which its readers, like the disciples and
other partners of Jesus that it introduces, succeed or fail in
being persuaded that its plot and cast re-enact and heighten
those of a model found in the Hebrew Bible. To the disciples
"the secret of the Kingdom of God" has already been given:
they know that 1 Kgs 17–2 Kgs 13 is the paradigm; they only
need to come to the insight that Jesus exceeds Elisha in a manner comparable to the way in which the latter exceeds his forerunner Elijah (8:14–21; see also 2.6 above). However, the case
has to be made more comprehensively and in greater detail for
those who are described as in one way or another moved by
Jesus' appearance, whether Joseph of Arimathea or the inquir-
ing Scripture scholar or, for that matter, other named and unnamed figures and groups portrayed in the gospel. Such persons
may appeal to Jesus for help, as the Synagogue president Jairus
(5:21–24/35–43) or the demon-possessed child's father (9:14–19)
do, or challenge him to debate, as the Pharisees (at times in association with other groups such as "some Scripture scholars"
or "Herodians") do in matters of ritual observance of purity, of
the permissibility of divorce, or the payment of tax to the Roman authorities (7:1–23, 10:2–12, 12:13–17). The nature of the
issues, be they pursued in an adversarial manner or not, iden-

tifies them as alive in intra-Israelite debates of the first century C.E., where appeals to Scripture are marshalled in support of claim and counter-claim (see especially Mk 10:2–12).

d. In this connection it is instructive that J. Louis Martyn, *History and Theology in the Fourth Gospel* (rev. ed., 1979), posits in the context of an assumed "expectation of a Mosaic Prophet-Messiah," the emergence of "an inner-synagogue group of Christian Jews" (117). He observes that the latter had to cope with fellow Jews not following Jesus, especially the teachers and theologians among them, who applied disciplinary pressures on their schismatic fellow Jews. One manner of avoiding confrontation was the way of "secret believers," that is, of those who

> are afraid to confess their faith in Jesus ... unless they are assured of convincing midrashic grounds for defense. For they quite naturally agree with the Jamnia Loyalists that the issue must be settled by exegesis. Unless they can defend their faith on the basis of midrash, they feel they must choose between hiding their faith and being excommunicated. [118]

Thus the fourth gospel may have arisen, Martyn argues, as an attempt not only to offer "powerful midrashic demonstration that Jesus fulfils the hope for the Prophet-Messiah like Moses," but also to "convince larger numbers of the common folk" — a route later chosen by Justin, too (118).

e. The exploration of the scriptural paradigms that shape the fourth gospel must be left to a projected, separate investigation. Suffice it to note that there is much evidence that Jn also is a literary conceptualization of Jesus' appearance, mission, and martyrdom in accord with biblical models that are more comprehensive than, but also partly identical with, the paradigm of Mk. Martyn's description of Jn as "powerful midrashic demonstration" (our reservations concerning the suitability of the term "midrash" notwithstanding) is not only analogous to the interpretation of Mk presented here but also may explain why in early Christian literature the gospel genre, at least in its later canonized form, appears only in the New Testament: Was it designed to persuade secret believers, that is, those who cherished the Hebrew Scriptures but were also sympathetic to the claims made by followers of Jesus concerning their master? *f.* With the increasing hardening of the division between synagogues and churches in the second century C.E. the need for such midrashic demonstration diminished and was replaced, to a certain extent, by the much more adversary argumentation of the literary "Adversus Judaeos" genre. By the same token, Mk together with the other gospels could now be read and understood, to use Papias' words, (only) as "all that he [Mark] remembered... of the things said and done by the Lord" (Eusebius, *Eccl. Hist.* III 39, 15). With the disappearance of the intended audience of the gospel the recognition of its scriptural code also had to disappear. The second gospel as well as its canonical counterparts could become the first and foundational part of the new Christian canon to the extent to which they were no more a continuation and heightening of the canon of the Synagogue's Bible.

9.2   The Predicament of Recent Research

A brief review of several recent discussions of the genre of the second gospel allows us to set the thesis of this study into the context of contemporary research.

   a. In his monograph entitled *The Oral and the Written Gospel* (1983), Werner Kelber has concentrated the discussion issuing from the form-, tradition-, and redaction-critical analyses of the gospel on the genesis of Mk in its written form and on the nature of its relationship to whatever oral traditions precede it. He sees Mk as a "linguistic artifact" (92) in its own right and argues that the form- and redaction-critical research of Bultmann and Marxsen ignore the thoroughgoing "transmutation" brought about by "a freezing of oral life into textual still life" (91). Such textualization is possible only through the introduction of "an ordering agent" (107) that proceeds to construct a narrative universe of its own. In other words, "a single organizing intellect" (114) brings into existence "not a copy of the Jesus of history, but rather an artistic creation" (116). The gospel of Mark, a work of compositional integrity and "constructive unity" (117), has its own new and distinctive literary identity. As such it is a parable writ large (215–220). Its intended meaning may be identified by an audience that follows "Jesus' way like the disciples to the very end" (123). The evangelist presents Jesus as "the parable of the kingdom of God" (220) and accomplishes that by "the comprehensive implementation of parabolic hermeneutic across the gospel" (219). Thus Kelber convincingly argues that Mark's miracle stories and parables serve "to shape the contours of a new and highly controversial reality" (111). He observes that "parables invite hearers into the story and through it to a story behind the story" (61), prompting them to search for "the formal, artistic principle determining the linguistic gestalt of the gospel" (117).

However, Kelber's search does not lead to the discovery of the literary form that defines the gospel in its entirety. Thus he must conclude that "parabolic disorientation" is Mark's last word because, "far from inviting us to settle for familiar, classical perspectives," the parable "shocks us out of them toward a new and unfamiliar logic" (129). The question is inescapable: Is "the story behind the story" of Mark (to use Kelber's formulation) destined to remain forever hidden? Is disorientation or disclosure the gospel's goal?

b. Frank Kermode's answer, in *The Genesis of Secrecy: On the Interpretation of Narrative* (1979), is similar to Kelber's in that it concludes that we find in the gospel as a whole "something irreducible, therefore perpetually to be interpreted; no secrets to be found out one by one, but Secrecy" (Kermode, 143). On the contrary, I submit that once those initiated into the secret have grasped the parable of the sower (Mk 4:3–8) as the master key (Mk 4:13), they are ready not only to understand the other parables (Mk 4:21–32; comp. 33–34), but also to be-

come active bearers of that insight. And it is this discovery that
they are sent to transmit parabolically, in the manner in which
it had been given to them. Thus the second gospel is indeed a
parabolic presentation. As such it moves its audience into the
very place that its author has vacated — the place of those who
find themselves engaged in the search for the story behind the
story.

c. In his article "Using Literary Criticism on the Gospels"
(1982), Robert Fowler argues that the historical-critical interpretation of the gospels has reached an impasse. He suggests
that what we now need is an interpretation of each gospel as a
work of literary art, shaped by its own, unique integrity. Fowler
shows for instance how "the usual scholarly accounting of the
two feeding stories" (Mk 6:32–44/8:1–9), "...rather than ex-
plaining the stories,...just explained them away" (628) as vari-
ants of the same traditional story. Thus he comes to insist that
"the literary critic, concerned with interpreting the Gospel as
an integral, literary whole, must deal with both feeding stories
with equal seriousness" (629). Fowler begins his essay with an
observation made by Norman Perrin, suggesting that the "evangelists are genuinely authors, authors using traditional material
but nonetheless authors: they write for a definite purpose, they
give their work a distinct and individual structure, they have
thematic concerns which they pursue, the characters in the stories they each tell function as protagonists in a plot...."

9.3 Mark's Bid for Biblical Legitimation

a. Ulrich Luz's review (1980) of three recent commentaries
on Mark (Rudolf Pesch, Joachim Gnilka, Walter Schmithals) is
provocatively titled "Markan Research in a Dead-End Street?"
He concludes that, while stocktaking is impossible at this time,
several postulates may be formulated for future research into
the origins of the gospels. Two of these are instructive in the
context of this study: the postulates of "simplicity" and of "continuity." He suggests that "simplicity" characterizes a hypothe-

sis that, rather than positing a complex process of composition, explains the genesis of the gospel on the basis of a simple organizing principle. This postulate as well as that of "continuity" are satisfied when it can be demonstrated that the works of the evangelists are, each in its own way, related to the Hebrew Scriptures as their primary matrix. In relation to the second gospel both postulates are satisfied by our thesis that the Elijah/Elisha Narrative in 1 Kgs 17–2 Kgs 13 supplies the scriptural code of Mark.

b. Why does Mark's work conceptualize and narratively present Jesus' appearance as conforming to and heightening a scriptural paradigm? I suggest that it is the evangelist's bid for a legitimation of the life and death of Jesus, the martyr from Galilee, through the medium of that authority that could be assumed to be that of its audience: the Hebrew Bible.

While a further discussion of the challenges faced by the evangelist is beyond the scope of this study, several aspects of the second gospel have been illumined.

First, our investigation not only shows that its composer is an author in the way in which Perrin and Kelber postulate, but also explains why the work is largely structured in plot and cast, as well as to a certain extent in narrated time, space, and motif selection and development, in the manner in which it presents itself — not to mention the comparability to its master narrative in volume.

Second, the argument of the gospel for the conception of Jesus' mission as following (and thus continuing into the time of the author) a biblical paradigm, as that ancient paradigm had done itself and in its own right, suggests the importance of what may be called "scriptural continuity," the presence and importance of other patterns such as those of Roman-Hellenistic master-disciple type casting notwithstanding.

Third, the findings have significance not only for the similarly structured gospels of Matthew and Luke in that they suggest the reason for the existence of the "synoptic" gospel type, but also for a similar analysis of the differently structured "Johannine" gospel (see my essay "Scriptural Coding in the Fourth Gospel").

Fourth, the study presents what may be identified as an aspect of "discourse analysis." It explores the gospel synchronically and thus not diachronically as form criticism, tradition criticism, and redaction criticism do. Our analysis lets itself be drawn into the discussion of "sources" only when the text itself implies that certain constraints are present; it does not assume a genesis in stages, moving from postulated small units alive in oral tradition through their oral or written clustering, editing, and framing to their eventual redaction into a sustained composition known as "gospel." Thus the question of the relation of discourse analysis to source analysis is posed in a new manner.

Finally, the study illustrates in an unexpected manner that the second gospel was conceived and designed to play its role within an *intra*-Israelite debate. It follows that reading it with the eyes of a community that had come to identify itself mostly over against its parent community (illustrated by such second century C.E. Christian voices as Papias) is a hermeneutic that is an understandable interpretive procedure from the second century C.E. onward but also a barrier for the access to the conceptual and literary creativity that generated Mk in the last third of the first century C.E., in the wake of the destruction of the Second Temple and more than a generation after Jesus' appearance.

Bibliography

Achtemeier, Paul J.

1970   "Toward the Isolation of Pre-Markan Miracle Cate-
     nae," *Journal of Biblical Literature* 89:265–291

1972   "The Origin and Function of the Pre-Markan Miracle
     Catenae," *Journal of Biblical Literature* 91:198–221

Baeck, Leo

1958   "The Gospel as Document of the History of the Jewish
     Faith," *Judaism and Christianity*. Philadelphia: Jewish
     Publication Society; 41–84

Betz, Otto

1960   *Offenbarung und Schriftforschung in der Qumransekte.*
     Wissenschaftliche Untersuchungen zum Neuen Testa-
     ment 6. Tübingen: Mohr

Bialik, H., and Revnizki, Y., eds.

1960   *A Book of Haggada*. Anthology of Stories from Talmud
     and Midrash (Hebrew). Tel Aviv: Debir

Blackmor, T. Gershon

1979   *Elijah and Elisha Motifs in the Gospels*. Rabbinic Or-
     dination Thesis. Cincinnati: Hebrew Union College–
     Jewish Institute of Religion

132   Bibliography

Boucher, Madeleine
    1977   *The Mysterious Parable. A Literary Study.* Catholic
                Biblical Quarterly Monograph Series 6. Washington:
                Catholic Biblical Association

Bowman, John
    1965   *The Gospel of Mark. The New Christian Jewish Pass-
                over Haggadah.* Studia Postbiblica 8. Leiden: Brill

Brodie, Thomas Louis
    1983a   "Greco-Roman Imitation of Texts as a Partial Guide
                to Luke's Use of Sources," *Essays on Luke/Acts,*
                Charles H. Talbert, ed. New York: Crossroad; 17–46
    1983b   "The Accusing and Stoning of Naboth (1 Kgs 21:8–13)
                as One Component of the Stephen Text (Acts 6:9–14;
                7:58a)," *Catholic Biblical Quarterly* 45:417–432
    1983c   "Luke 7:36–50 as an Internalization of 2 Kings 4:1–
                37: A Study in Luke's Use of Rhetorical Imitation,"
                Biblica 64:457–485

Brown, Raymond E.
    1971   "Jesus and Elisha," *Perspective* XII:85–104

Danby, Herbert, ed.
    1933   *The Mishnah.* London: Oxford University Press

Derrett, J. Duncan M.
    1985   *The Making of Mark. The Scriptural Bases of the Ear-
                liest Gospel.* Shipston-on-Stour: Drinkwater

Elliger, K., and Rudolph, W.
    1977   *Biblia Hebraica Stuttgartensia.* Stuttgart: Deutsche
                Bibelstiftung

Epstein, I., ed. *The Babylonian Talmud.* London: Soncino

Fiebig, Paul.

1911   *Jüdische Wundergeschichten des neutestamentlichen Zeitalters.* Tübingen: Mohr

1912   *Die Gleichnisreden Jesu im Lichte der rabbinischen Gleichnisse des neutestamentlichen Zeitalters.* Tübingen: Mohr

1925   *Der Erzählungsstil der Evangelien.* Leipzig: Hinrichs'sche Verlagsbuchhandlung

Fowler, Robert

1982   "Using Literary Criticism on the Gospels," *Christian Century* 99/19:626–629

Ginzberg, Louis, ed.,

1909–38   *The Legends of the Jews.* 7 vols. Philadelphia: Jewish Publication Society

Güttgemanns, Erhardt.

1979   "Die Funktion der Erzählung im Judentum als Frage an das christliche Verständnis der Evangelien," *Linguistica Biblica* 46:6–61

Haag, Herbert

1968   *Bibel-Lexikon.* 2nd ed. Einsiedeln: Benziger Verlag

Habermann, A. M.

1959   *The Scrolls from the Judean Desert* (Hebrew). Machbaroth Lesifruth Publishing House

Hartmann, Gerhard

1936   *Der Aufbau des Markusevangeliums.* Münster: Aschendorff

Hatch, Edwin, and Redpath, Henry A.

1897   *A Concordance to the Septuagint.* Oxford: Clarendon

134   Bibliography

Heinemann, Isaak
   1970   The Ways of Hagadda (Hebrew). Jerusalem: Magnes

Kadushin, Max
   1952   The Rabbinic Mind. New York: Jewish Theological
             Seminary

Kee, Howard Clark
   1977   Community of the New Age: Studies in Mark's Gospel.
             Philadelphia: Westminster

Kelber, Werner H.
   1983   The Oral and the Written Gospel: The Hermeneutics of
             Speaking and Writing in the Synoptic Tradition, Mark,
             Paul and Q. Philadelphia: Fortress

Kennedy, George A.
   1984   New Testament Interpretation Through Rhetorical Crit-
             icism. Chapel Hill and London: University of North
             Carolina Press

Kermode, Frank
   1979   The Genesis of Secrecy: On the Interpretation of Nar-
             rative. Cambridge, Mass., and London: Harvard Uni-
             versity Press

Lake, Kirsopp, and Oulton, J.E.L.
   1965-64   Eusebius. The Ecclesiastical History. 2 vols. Loeb Se-
             ries. Cambridge, Mass., and London: Harvard Univer-
             sity Press

Lisowsky, Gerhard
   1958   Concordantiae Veteris Testamenti. Stuttgart: Privileg-
             ierte Württembergische Bibelanstalt

Lohse, Eduard, ed.
   1964   Die Texte aus Qumran. Munich: Kösel

Luz, Ulrich

1980   "Markusforschung in der Sackgasse," *Theologische Literaturzeitung* 105:641–655

Mandelkern, Solomon.

1971   *Veteris Testamenti Concordantiae Hebraicae atque Chaldaicae.* Reprint edition. Jerusalem and Tel Aviv: Schocken

Martyn, J. Louis

1979   *History and Theology in the Fourth Gospel.* rev. ed. Nashville: Abingdon

Marxsen, Willy

1969   *Mark the Evangelist. Studies on the Redaction History of the Gospel.* Trans. J. Boyce and others. Nashville: Abingdon

Nestle, Eberhard; Nestle, Erwin; Aland, Kurt; Aland, Barbara

1979   *Novum Testamentum Graece.* 26th ed. Stuttgart: Deutsche Bibelstiftung

Patte, Daniel

1975   *Early Jewish Hermeneutic in Palestine.* Society of Biblical Literature Dissertation Series. Missoula: Scholars Press

Petersen, Norman

1978   "Point of View in Mark's Narrative," *Semeia 12,* 97–121

Rahlfs, Alfred

1952   *Septuaginta.* 5th ed. Stuttgart: Privilegierte Württembergische Bibelanstalt

Robbins, Vernon K.

1984   *Jesus the Teacher: A Socio-Rhetorical Interpretation of Mark.* Philadelphia: Fortress

Robinson, J.A.T.

1958   "Elijah, John and Jesus: An Essay in Detection," *New Testament Studies* 4:263–281

Roth, Wolfgang

1987   "Scriptural Coding in the Fourth Gospel," *Biblical Research* 32:6–29

Schmidt, Karl Ludwig

1919   *Der Rahmen der Geschichte Jesu*. Berlin: Trowitzsch

Scholem, Gershom

1962   "Revelation and Tradition as Religious Categories in Judaism," *The Messianic Idea in Judaism*. New York: Schocken; 282–303

Seeligmann, I. L.

1953   "Voraussetzungen der Midraschexegese," *Vetus Testamentum Supplement* I:150–181

Silberman, Lou H.

1961   "Unriddling the Riddle: A Study in the Structure and Language of the Habakkuk Pesher," *Revue de Qumran* 11:322–364

Suter, David Winston

1979   *Tradition and Composition in the Parables of Enoch*. Society of Biblical Literature Dissertation Series. Missoula: Scholars Press

Thackeray, H. St. J., and others

1926–65   *Josephus*. 9 vols. Loeb Series. Cambridge, Mass., and London: Harvard University Press

Weeden, Theodore J.

1971   *Mark — Traditions in Conflict*. Philadelphia: Fortress

Wilder, Amos N.

1964   *Early Christian Rhetoric. The Language of the Gospel.*
        London: SCM Press

Wrede, William

1901   *Das Messiasgeheimnis in den Evangelien.* Göttingen:
        Vandenhoeck & Ruprecht

Index of Scriptural References

Index of Extrabiblical Texts

Index of Authors

Made in the USA
Coppell, TX
16 February 2020